THE IRON QUEEN

A Novel of Boudica

L.D. GOFFIGAN

This is a work of historical fiction. Apart from the well-known actual people, events, and locales that figure in the narrative, all incidents are either products of the author's imagination or used fictitiously. Any resemblance to current events or locales, or to living persons, is entirely coincidental.

Copyright © 2018 by L.D. Goffigan

All rights reserved.

This book or any portion thereof may not be reproduced, or stored in a retrieval system, or transmitted in any form or by any means, electronic, mechanical, photocopying, recording, or otherwise, without the express written permission of the publisher.

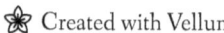 Created with Vellum

LIST OF CHARACTERS

The Iceni and other native tribes
- Boudica - daughter of the chieftain Antedios
- Antedios - chieftain of the Iceni
- Prasutagus - noble / Antedios's unofficial heir
- Kensa - Boudica's foster sister
- Rozen - Boudica's foster mother
- Mael - chief druid priest
- Judoc - warrior
- Cadell - Trinovantes chieftain
- Cartimandua - Brigantes queen
- Yannik - chieftain of the Cantiaci tribe
- Gael - chieftain of the Belgae tribe
- Corentin - chieftain of the Durotriges tribe

The Romans
- Gaius Suetonius Paulinus - Roman governor

LIST OF CHARACTERS

 Aulus Plautius - Roman governor
 Catus Decianus - Roman procurator
 Quintus Petillius Cerialis - Roman general
 Tertius - Roman soldier
 Aelius - Roman soldier

Gods and Goddesses
 Andraste - Celtic war goddess
 Damara - Celtic fertility goddess
 Garmangabis - Celtic goddess of fortune
 Fortuna - Roman goddess of fortune

PROLOGUE

There lived a beast called Rome.

A savage and ravenous beast, Rome had conquered most of the known world. It then turned hungry eyes across the great waters, to the wild lands of the north...

To the lands they called Britannia.

Native tribes of the land tried to fight back, to fell the beast, but they were all defeated. And like many others before them, they were forced to make an alliance.

But Rome would create a beast of its own making... one that would cripple the knees of the mighty empire.

- Bard from the Caledonian tribe
89 CE

I

47 CE

The Chieftain's Daughter

I

It was the first day of Beltaine; a time when the cool days turned warm, the nights grew shorter, and the herdsmen drove their cattle out to the pastures. To celebrate the dawn of a new season, the men and women of the Iceni tribe set ritual fires ablaze throughout the fields surrounding their village. Smoke billowed from the openings of thatch-roofed roundhouses throughout the village, and the scent of roasted meats filled the air, mingling with the acrid flames of the fires.

In the village square, women carried baskets of fruit, spiced breads, and jugs of mead and ale to share with their neighbors. Other villagers chanted prayers of worship to the gods as they encircled the fires with clutched hands; it was said the gods grew restless when the seasons changed, and the prayers and fires appeased them.

Amid the festivities, a young woman snuck out of

the village. She was in her seventeenth year, the early blush of womanhood. She'd braided her long, flame-colored hair into a single plait and tucked it into the back of her tunic, a plainer tunic than she often wore for tribal festivals. As daughter of the chieftain Antedios, she was expected to wear her finest on days like today. Her attendants would dress her in a fine silk tunic with a tartan cloak of green and lavender, fastened with a golden brooch. They'd braid her hair into three long plaits and bind it at her nape with a golden clip, before placing a bronze or gold torc around her arm, signaling her royal status.

But for now, Boudica wanted to avoid notice. She'd waved away her attendants and dressed herself this morning, telling them she'd change into her finery before the ritual feast that evening.

She kept her head bowed as she made her way into the vast woodlands that surrounded the village like a beast encroaching upon its prey. Her father once told her that the gods gifted the lands surrounding the village to their people, from the fertile fields to the woodlands, filled with sacred groves where white-robed druid priests held sacred rituals.

As she ventured into the woodlands, the scent of the ritual fires grew faint. Here, there was only the fragrant scent of earth, damp from rains that fell the day before. Boudica inhaled, allowing her shoulders to relax. The forest was her place of peace, of refuge. When she was a girl, she often got lost amid the labyrinth of trees; her father had to send the best hunters of the tribe to track her down.

She moved past the familiar landscape of alder and hawthorn trees, their winding branches arching toward the sky as if beseeching the gods, stopping only when she reached a small clearing.

Boudica smiled at the sight of the young man who waited for her there. Besides Kensa, the girl she'd grown up with and considered a sister, Prasutagus was her only true friend in the tribe. A strange rush flowed through her at the sight of him.

She'd known Prasutagus since they were both children. He was one of the few men of the tribe who towered above Boudica. The soft features that defined his once boyish face had sharpened into handsome, angular features—he had amber eyes, a strong jaw, an aquiline nose and a prominent brow, all framed by dark, wavy hair. She'd seen some women of the tribe looking at him with desire; he was in his nineteenth year and would soon marry.

A sharp, unfamiliar emotion filled her at the thought of Prasutagus marrying, but she pushed the feeling away. It didn't matter who or when Prasutagus wed. She herself never wished to marry, though she knew her father would give her no choice in the matter.

"I'm sorry it took me some time to get here. Rozen had her eyes on me while I helped with the feast," Boudica said, as Prasutagus knelt to pick up a sword that rested at the base of a birch tree.

Irritation skittered through her at the memory. Fostering was the practice of the tribe; Rozen had fostered her since she was a girl of seven, after the mother who birthed Boudica joined the gods. Rozen was the closest person she had to a mother and knew Boudica well. She seemed to sense that Boudica was biding her time to sneak away and kept giving her more tasks.

"I wasn't waiting long," Prasutagus said, giving her a light smile as he handed her the sword.

Boudica took it and a sense of strength coursed through her, the same feeling that consumed her whenever she held a weapon in her hands. She'd practiced fighting with all manner of weapons: daggers, axes, spears—but her favorite was the sword.

Prasutagus faced her, moving into a fighting stance as he gripped his own sword. Boudica expelled a breath, whispering a silent prayer to Andraste, the warrior goddess, before lunging forward.

Exhilaration filled Boudica as she whirled and parried around him with practiced ease, meeting each of his sword thrusts with her own. She lost herself in the thrill of fighting, her heartbeat thudding in her ears as steadily as the clappers that accompanied the tribe into battle. She lived for these moments when she could sneak away from her duties and pretend to be a warrior.

Boudica had seen her first battle during her ninth year. It was the custom of the tribe to take families to witness battles, lining them up in wagons at the rear of the battlefield to watch the tribesmen in their glory. Awe had flowed through Boudica as she watched the tribal warriors leap onto their enemies with savage grace, their cries of triumph echoing throughout the fields whenever they won a battle. The warriors were the nobles of her tribe; they sat at her father's side during feasts, the bards told tales of their feats in battle, and her father rewarded them with fine homes and lands. There were even women warriors, and they were just as vicious as the men in combat. Years ago, one female warrior, Jacca, had taken more heads in battle against a rival tribe than any of the male warriors. Her father had given her a large haunch of a boar as a prize.

Though Boudica wanted nothing more than to become a warrior, Antedios forbade it. She was his only surviving child; two sons had died as babes, and one daughter died with his last wife in childbirth. Antedios wanted her to wed a noble of his choosing, to bear sons who would continue his line and become chieftains and warriors. He refused to even let her practice; Prasutagus was the only one who'd practice with her, risking her father's wrath. It was why she had to sneak away to fight.

But Boudica was determined to convince her father to allow her to fight, and then she would become even greater than Jacca. The bards would describe her might in battle, and when it was her time to join the gods, her tribe would remember her; they would chant her name with reverence for years to come.

The metallic clash of Prasutagus's sword against hers pulled Boudica from her thoughts, and she parried, thrusting forward with her blade. Their swords met in midair, at a stalemate.

Boudica's eyes met Prasutagus's across their blades. As his gaze settled on hers, a flood of warmth filled her. She hated the hot flush that spread across her cheeks and lowered her eyes.

"Do you yield?" Boudica asked, concentrating on the hilt of her sword.

"I yield."

To her surprise, Prasutagus lowered his sword. He never yielded with such ease.

He stepped forward, his eyes roaming over her flushed face. Boudica's heart picked up its pace, her breath catching in her throat at his sudden nearness.

Prasutagus opened his mouth to speak, but faltered at the sight of something behind her.

"Boudica!"

Boudica whirled, a guilty flush spreading across her face. Kensa hovered behind them at the edge of the clearing, clutching a basket of hawthorn flowers, her eyebrows knitted together in a frown.

"Rozen's looking for you," Kensa said, her gaze sliding past her to Prasutagus with vague suspicion. "We have more to prepare for tonight's feast."

Boudica's shoulders sank. She'd thought her duties were complete; she'd looked forward to sword practice all day. She considered asking Kensa to lie for her, to tell Rozen she'd been unable to find her.

"She'll come looking for you herself," Kensa warned, discerning her thoughts.

"We can practice again tomorrow," Prasutagus said from behind her.

Boudica turned to him with a nod, though disappointment settled onto her shoulders like a mighty rock. She didn't meet his eyes as she handed him her sword, recalling the moment Kensa had interrupted. Why had he approached her? What was he going to say—or do?

She felt his gaze on her back as she left with Kensa, forcing the questions from her mind. Prasutagus was her friend, he'd been her friend since she was young and nothing more.

"Rozen hates it when you sneak off to fight. She'll tell your father," Kensa said, linking her arm through Boudica's as they made their way out of the forest. Kensa lowered her voice to match Rozen's stern tone. "'A chieftain's daughter only duty is to have strong sons . . . not sully herself with the sword.' You know the chieftain will never allow you to be a warrior."

Boudica scowled. "Father should let me fight. I'm better than most warriors of the tribe."

"Should I tell him that?" Kensa asked, her tone teasing, and Boudica's bravado slipped. Her father had earned his place as chieftain by killing a rival warrior. He stood taller than all the men of the tribe; even the mightiest warrior dared not cross him.

Boudica had tried arguing with him only once about her desire to become a warrior; he'd silenced her with just a look from his hard green eyes.

"No," Boudica said hastily, and Kensa chuckled. She glanced back at Prasutagus, who lingered in the clearing.

"Your betrothed will be chosen soon," Kensa said, her tone heavy with meaning.

"Prasutagus is my friend," Boudica said, avoiding Kensa's perceptive gaze. "No one else will fight with me. They're all afraid of my father."

The teasing glint remained in Kensa's eyes, but she dropped the matter as they made their way back to the village.

Reveling villagers filled the central square, drunk from the ale they'd consumed. Boudica and Kensa had to weave around them as they neared the larger aristocratic roundhouses situated just beyond the village square.

Dread coiled around Boudica like a forest snake as they approached their home. She feared that Rozen would glean she'd snuck off to fight with Prasutagus, disobeying her orders. Antedios loved Prasutagus like a son, he'd been close to his father, and there were rumors he wanted Prasutagus to succeed him as chieftain of the tribe. But her father would punish Prasutagus if he found out he was helping her fight . . . and he'd take her weapons away.

"I won't tell Rozen you were fighting," Kensa said gently, as Boudica tensed. She gave Boudica's hand a reassuring squeeze. "But stop leaving me with all the chores."

Boudica gave her an apologetic smile. "All right. I'm sorry."

Boudica's smile froze on her face when their foster mother stepped out of the roundhouse they approached. Rozen looked just as she had when Boudica first came to live with her: hair as dark as a raven's feathers, sharp gray eyes, fine, delicate features. The only difference now were the strands of gray woven throughout her hair and the faint wrinkles around her eyes.

"Where did you run off to, child?" Rozen demanded.

Boudica hated when Rozen called her a child; many women were married and swollen with babes of their own by her age. But she didn't dare say anything defiant, not with the hard look on Rozen's face.

Kensa stepped forward, holding up her basket of flowers.

"She was gathering hawthorn to wear in her hair for the feast tonight."

For a tense moment, Rozen studied Boudica, as if trying to discern the truth of Kensa's words. Boudica held her gaze, hoping her guilt didn't show.

"Very well," Rozen murmured, stepping aside to wave them in. "Next time you tell me where you're going on days like today."

Rozen turned to step back inside. Boudica gave Kensa another smile, this one grateful.

But as she entered Rozen's home, a pang of bitterness pierced her as Kensa's words swirled in her mind. *The chieftain will never allow you to be a warrior.*

2

As the light faded from the sky, Boudica entered her father's home with the nobles of the tribe for the ritual feast. She took in his massive home as she sat on a pile of animal furs before a low table. She'd visited her father's home many times, but its grandeur always struck her.

As chieftain, Antedios had the grandest roundhouse in the village. Wooden rafters supported the massive, high-sloping thatched roof, the opening revealing the starry night sky above. The firelight from the central hearth danced off the lime-washed daub walls. Servants and attendants had placed roasted meats on hot stones next to the hearth to keep them warm, and their succulent fragrance filled the interior of the home.

Around her, guests sat on animal skins and furs on the clay floors. Heaped on the low wooden tables before them were plates filled with roasted fish, salted pork—pulled from the winter stores—and bread. Attendants milled around, filling the guests' cups with spiced wine and ale. In the far corner of the home, several minstrels sang, their soft voices blending with the strums of their lyres.

As Kensa and Rozen settled in next to her, Boudica reached for a piece of salted pork on the bronze plate before her, savoring the salty texture of the meat. She glanced across the wide expanse of the home at Antedios, who sat at the head table next to Mael, the chief druid priest and his close personal advisor.

Even seated, her father was intimidating. He was strong and broad-shouldered, sporting the rich tartan cloak, golden torc, and long mustache of a chieftain. His hair, the same flame-colored hue as hers, seemed darker in the dim firelight of the home, and his green eyes were thoughtful as he spoke to Mael in low tones.

Mael's dark gaze settled on her, and she averted her eyes. Mael had always frightened her. He rarely spoke, and his black eyes were unreadable. Not much was known about him; rumors abounded that he'd trained at the isle of Mona, the headquarters of the druids in the north, for twenty summers. A former chieftain had chosen him as high priest of the tribe before she was born, and her father trusted his council. Whenever there was a crime committed by a member of the tribe and the nobles couldn't agree upon a punishment, it was Mael they went to for a decision; he knew all the tribal laws by heart. It was even said that he had foreseen the coming of the Romans, those armored men from the territory beyond the great waters that surrounded their lands.

The hum of conversation ceased when Antedios got to his feet, his stature seeming to consume the entirety of the grand home as his gaze swept over every guest. Boudica stilled when Antedios briefly met her gaze; he rarely acknowledged her during public feasts and it was disconcerting when he did.

"Should we begin with the first combat challenge of the night?" he asked, turning his attention to the other guests, his booming voice firm and commanding.

The guests cheered, and Boudica joined in. Anticipation filled her; watching the combat challenges was her favorite part of the ritual feasts. They presented the opportunity for the strongest warriors of the tribe to prove their strength against each other.

Antedios turned to the opposite corner of the room, gesturing to two warriors. Boudica recognized the two men, Judoc and Doane. They were two of the tribe's strongest warriors, neither of whom had ever lost a challenge. Tribal tattoos and blue war paint made from woad covered their flesh, giving them the fierce appearance of beasts, their eyes shining in the glow of firelight.

At Antedios's signal, they walked to the center of

the home. They moved into fighting stances, and after a tense moment of silence, they lunged at each other.

The guests erupted into cheers and tribal battle cries as the men fought with their bare hands, slamming each other to the ground, each battling for dominance. It seemed they were evenly matched until Judoc pinned Doane beneath him. He wrapped his hands around Doane's throat, tightening his grip, as the cheers of the guests rose to a crescendo.

"Gods," Kensa murmured. "I can't watch."

But Boudica couldn't take her eyes off of them. Most combat challenges didn't end with deaths, but for the ones that did, Antedios rewarded the warrior who won with a sizable prize—stores of meat for his household to use during the long winters, weapons, a larger home, or even lands. She'd seen only a few warriors go to their deaths during combat challenges, and she made certain to watch their eyes as they drew their last breath. If she was to be a warrior, it was important to not look away from death.

What are their last thoughts? she'd wonder as she watched the life drain from their eyes. *What do they see before they go to the gods?*

She kept her eyes trained on Doane's final struggles as Judoc tightened his grip. Doane's blue eyes went hazy and unfocused before he stilled, drawing his last ragged breath.

As soon as Doane went still, Judoc got to his feet, holding his hands above his head, bellowing out a triumphant cry. The guests cheered, chanting his name and shouting more tribal cries.

Antedios gestured for Judoc to come sit at his side, an honor only given to winners of combat challenges. As two attendants hurried forward to remove Doane's body, Antedios announced Judoc's prize: Doane's larger home and his farm, along with an extra store of meats.

Antedios moved to the center of the home, and the guests once again fell silent.

"Who wishes to take part in the next challenge?" he asked. "Who wishes to fight . . . me?"

An awed hush fell. Boudica stared at her father, stunned. Though her father was a strong fighter, he seldom participated in combat challenges. When he did, no one was allowed to kill him. But that didn't mean he couldn't kill his challenger.

No one volunteered. Many even lowered their eyes. Boudica looked around, her heart hammering. If her father saw how strong she'd become, perhaps he'd consent to her becoming a warrior. Perhaps he wouldn't make her wed.

She scrambled to her feet, stepping out from behind her table to move to the center of the home. She met her father's gaze, fighting to keep her voice steady as she spoke.

"I'll fight you, Father."

Many of the guests let out startled gasps. Boudica briefly met Prasutagus's gaze; he sat with other male nobles on the opposite side of the home. Panic flared in his expression, and he subtly shook his head.

Boudica tore her gaze away from him, holding her head high as she faced her father, whose expression was unreadable.

Amid the stunned silence, Rozen scrambled to her feet, giving Antedios an apologetic look.

"Come and sit down, child," Rozen hissed, grabbing her arm.

But Boudica didn't budge from Rozen's insistent tugging, her gaze trained on her father, her heart thundering in her chest like the bolts in the sky that signaled the coming rains.

"Boudica," Rozen repeated, "come sit, child."

"Sit, Rozen," Antedios said, his gaze never leaving Boudica's face. "If my daughter wants to fight . . . I will allow her to do so."

A ripple of surprise and excitement flowed through Boudica, followed by a trickle of fear. Her father was a fierce fighter, she didn't come near his strength. But she pushed away her fear. Her father wouldn't harm her.

Antedios gestured to a hovering attendant, who handed them both swords. He clutched the sword and faced her, as still as a waiting hawk. Boudica felt every eye in the home on her.

She closed her eyes, silently issuing a prayer to Andraste, before lunging forward with her sword. Antedios easily parried her first blow. She tried again, and this time her sword met his.

Excitement roiled through her as they began to fight, their clashing blades the only sound in the hushed home. Pride swelled within her as she kept up with her father's movements, meeting each of his blows with her own. She may have imagined it, but at one point she saw a glint of admiration in his eyes. He had to see how strong she was, how worthy she was of becoming a warrior.

But as her confidence reached its peak, she missed a vital parry. Antedios moved swiftly, knocking away her sword with his own. She tried to reach for it, but he shoved her back with the butt of his sword.

Boudica stumbled, falling onto her back. Searing pain coursed through her at her body's impact with the hard clay floor, and she let out a cry.

Her father stepped forward. Panic rose in her chest, and she twisted to reach for her sword, but Antedios kicked it out of her grasp. Boudica met his eyes; their green depths were now filled with a storm of fury. He raised his sword and stabbed it down, only an inch from her skull, pinning one of her braids to the ground.

Fear gripped her; there was no mercy in Antedios's eyes. He tossed his sword aside, placing his bare foot on her throat and pressing down.

Terror paired with shock skittered through Boudica as she tried to twist out of his grasp. But he forced her still, his foot cutting off her air. The guests were stunned silent as they watched; the crackling fire of the hearth and Boudica's desperate gasps for air the only sounds that filled the home.

"You've been fighting, though I forbid it," Antedios said, his voice low, though it vibrated with fury. "I have told you of your duties to the tribe, yet you disregard them like a spoiled child."

He leaned down, lowering his voice. Boudica fought to breathe, desperate for air, but he kept his foot firm against her throat.

"If you desire to be a warrior, you must learn humility. And that means obeying orders, even ones you do not like. You must learn to think; it is what great warriors do. Foolish impulsiveness will only get you killed."

Antedios lifted his foot, stepping back. Boudica sat up, coughing and gasping for air. He squatted down to her level, pressing his hand over her hammering heart. Hot fury and humiliation flooded her as she glared at him.

"That rage that's scorching your insides like fire?" he whispered. "When the time is right, use it to your advantage. It is best to know when to fight, daughter. When to win."

He held her gaze for a long moment before he straightened, turning to face the hushed crowd.

"Bring forth the bards. It's time for some tales, is it not?"

The guests shouted their agreement. Boudica stumbled to her feet, shame flooding every part of her as she stumbled out of her father's home.

Cool night air prickled at her skin as she hurried across the village square, away from the clamor of the ritual feast. The square was quiet now; the outside festivities had concluded, and the villagers were now in their smaller homes, smoke from their hearth fires billowing to the sky from openings in the thatched roofs.

"Boudica, wait—" Prasutagus called from behind her.

Boudica didn't stop; she wanted to be left alone. She continued out of the village, not looking back, though she heard Prasutagus's footfalls behind her as she made her way to the sanctuary of the forest. She didn't stop until she reached the same clearing where they'd fought earlier. Moonlight now illuminated the clearing, though the surrounding trees cast ominous shadows with their twisting branches.

Boudica moved toward a fallen tree and sat, placing her bare feet in the cool stream that snaked through it. Prasutagus sat down next to her, and a long silence stretched before she spoke. Only moments earlier she'd wanted to be alone, but she was now grateful for Prasutagus's quiet, calming presence.

"Father hates me because I'm his daughter and not his son," she said, pain piercing her stomach like an arrow. "He's always hated me. That's why he sent me away to live with Rozen after Mother joined the gods."

"Your father doesn't hate you, Boudica," he gently returned.

"You saw him back there," she whispered, blinking back tears. She looked up at him, humiliation coursing through her at the memory. "He took pleasure in hurting me."

"He knows how impulsive you can be. I think . . . he was guiding you. In his own way. My father took me hunting when I was still a boy. Left me in the middle of these woods in the dead of night. No food, no water. I had to find my way back to the village on my own."

Surprise filled her at his words. He'd always told her he didn't remember his father, who'd died in battle with a rival tribe when he was young. Prasutagus's father had been a great warrior; many believed that if he'd not died, he would have become chieftain instead of Antedios.

Tumult entered Prasutagus's eyes as he gazed down at the dark stream as if lost in the memory.

"It was a harsh lesson. But now I know these woods like every strand of my bed furs. Your father loves you, Boudica." He met her eyes, reaching out to touch her cheek. It was a brief touch, but enough to send a blazing heat careening through her, like the heat from the ritual fires. "You are loved."

His eyes held hers, filled with a longing she'd never seen before. For a moment, Boudica forgot all about her father and her humiliation. There was only the heat of Prasutagus's gaze on her skin, the thundering of her heart, the sudden dryness of her throat.

But Prasutagus looked away, and the moment passed. In the distance, the mingled voices of female guests leaving Antedios's home reached her ears. Most of the male nobles would remain in her father's home all night, drinking and boasting and fighting until they fell into long drunken sleeps on their animal pelts.

"We should return," Prasutagus said. "Your father will be worried. He will," he said, at the look of disbelief she gave him. "I remember when you disappeared into the forest once as a girl. I'd never seen such fear in his eyes as when he sent his men to find you."

Boudica didn't believe her father could fear anything, much less the demise of his troublesome and defiant daughter, but she said nothing.

Prasutagus helped her to her feet, and she noticed that he took care to not let his hand linger on hers. A stab of hurt pierced her, and she wondered if she'd perhaps imagined the heated moment they'd just shared.

"Your stitching is wrong. Start over," Rozen snapped.

Boudica's hand stilled on her stitching and she bit

back a defiant reply. It was early the next morning; Boudica and Kensa had barely finished eating the first meal of the day when Rozen put them to work on their embroidery.

Rozen had scolded her when she'd returned from the forest last night with Prasutagus, telling her how foolishly she'd behaved at the feast.

Boudica had taken the scolding in silence, ignoring Kensa's sympathetic stare as she trained her focus on the ground. She knew it would make things worse if she tried to defend herself; she'd only offered a quiet apology.

"I'm sorry, Rozen," she said now, hoping that her continued submissiveness would make Rozen forgive her sooner.

Rozen's gray eyes softened as they landed on her, but her mouth tightened, and she retreated to the loom in the corner where she was weaving a cloak.

Stifling a frustrated sigh, Boudica undid the stitching. Though Rozen had put out the hearth's fire, its ashes still floated through the air, pricking her nose, along with the scent of salted meats that hung in the rear of the home.

Rozen had given Boudica and Kensa two completed wool tunics to embroider, their tartan pattern made from earth dyes; leaves and woad. Boudica glanced at Kensa's finely stitched tunic with envy. Kensa had trained with several noblewomen in the practice of looming and embroidery; her clothing always came out superior to anything Boudica could make. Boudica had not yet trained in the craft though she was expected to; noblewomen had to enter their marriages with some knowledge of a household craft.

"It's a gift for Arthek," Kensa said, beaming with pride as she noticed Boudica's eyes on the tunic.

Boudica had noticed the shy and furtive looks between Kensa and Arthek, the eldest son of a farmer. With Kensa's long golden hair and eyes the color of chestnuts, many men of the tribe eyed her. Kensa would make a prized bride not just for her beauty, but her sizable dowry. Kensa was the daughter of a deceased noble warrior, and her mother had died when she was young; it was Antedios who would approve her choice of husband.

"Arthek wants me for his wife," Kensa continued, a blush staining her cheeks. "I know he's not noble . . . but Rozen will speak to your father on my behalf. Arthek has saved his wages; he'll pay my dowry."

Boudica forced a smile, returning her attention to her embroidery. Antedios was strict when it came to tradition and upholding the rules of the tribe; she doubted he'd allow Kensa to choose a husband who wasn't noble. But she had no desire to dash the light of happiness that shone in Kensa's eyes.

"I'm happy for you," Boudica said.

"I wonder who your father will choose for you," Kensa mused. "He loves Prasutagus like a son; he would be suitable. And it's likely he'll be the next chieftain. But there are also the warrior nobles—Winoc or Perig."

Heat flared within her at Kensa's mention of Prasutagus, but she kept her gaze trained on her stitching.

"I don't wish to wed, Kensa," she said, keeping her voice low, hoping that Rozen wasn't listening to their conversation.

"It is not your wishes that matter, child," Rozen said. Boudica frowned; Rozen had the ears of an owl. "You should thank the gods that you are royal, Boudica. You'll have servants tending to you and your household. Most of the tribe spend their lives toiling in the fields. My husband and I plowed our fields from morning to night. After he joined the gods, I had to do it on my own. I no longer bled; I couldn't be a useful wife to another husband. If the chieftain hadn't raised my rank and let me foster two noble girls . . . I don't know if I'd have survived. Look at me, child."

Boudica reluctantly turned to face Rozen, who dropped her hands from her loom and leaned forward, her gray eyes intense.

"You need to learn your place in this tribe. And be grateful for it."

"Yes, Rozen," Boudica murmured, returning her focus to her stitching, taking great effort to push aside the defiance simmering within her.

"Boudica—" Rozen started, her voice stern, but she abruptly fell silent.

Boudica stilled. Outside, she could hear

marching feet and horse hooves approaching. Unease rippled through her.

She turned to face Rozen, who'd gone pale.

"The Romans," Rozen whispered, her body tensing with dread.

3

Boudica had seen Roman soldiers only once in her life. Four summers ago, they'd marched into the village, and she'd taken in the strange men and their clothing with wide eyes: the brass helmets and silver, segmented body armor, the tunics which were the color of blood. She'd listened, trembling, as the Roman warriors—they called themselves soldiers—spoke an odd tongue to her father and the nobles. And then her father had done something she'd never seen him do before; he'd knelt before the lead warrior, whom the Romans called a general. The general had looked down upon her father and the other members of the tribe with disdain, as if they were mere insects beneath his feet.

She'd not understood the words the Roman general had spoken to the tribe, but she later overheard Rozen discussing them with other noblewomen. The Romans were to rule over their tribe and other tribes of the surrounding lands. Her father had vowed to not rise against them or their chieftain, whom the Romans called emperor, in order to avoid bloodshed.

"The Romans take pride in their lands, yet they devour the lands that surround their own like hungry wolves," Rozen had said, anger filling her eyes.

Since that first visit, the Romans had not visited their village—other than the soldiers they sent to collect taxes. Her father continued to rule their tribe, and Boudica sometimes forgot that foreigners were even in their land.

What are they doing here now? she wondered with worry. Boudica exchanged a nervous look with Kensa as they trailed Rozen to the doorway.

Boudica watched Antedios step out of the chieftain's home to greet the detachment of Roman soldiers. If their arrival surprised him, he didn't show it; his expression was neutral but pleasant. Several of his advisors and guards flanked him, including Mael and the warrior who'd won last night's combat challenge, Judoc.

The two leaders of the detachment dismounted from their horses. One was a stout, balding man with cold dark eyes; he gave the villagers a dismissive look. The other leader was tall and broad-shouldered, with short-cropped, blond hair and eyes the color of the sky.

"Stand back, girls," Rozen hissed, moving to stand protectively in front of them. But Boudica and Kensa remained by the doorway, peeking around Rozen as the two leaders addressed Antedios and the gathered villagers.

"Who are they?" Boudica asked Rozen.

"The tall one is the Roman governor, Aulus Plautius. The second one is Catus Decianus."

It was Aulus Plautius who spoke, speaking loud enough so that all the gathered villagers could hear. He spoke in their tongue and not his native Latin, though his words were heavily accented.

"The western tribes have staged rebellions against Roman settlements. To prevent further violence, the Emperor has decreed we take all weapons held by the tribes in this region."

Disbelief coursed through Boudica, and an outcry arose from the villagers. The Roman soldiers immediately surrounded their leaders in a protective formation. Antedios gestured for the villagers to remain calm before turning back to face Aulus.

"We gave you our word not to rise against Rome," Antedios said. "Our word is law. We took no part in those rebellions."

"We gave you an order," Catus said, his voice rising. "You will adhere—"

"King Antedios, this need not be difficult. This is temporary, until we're certain there will be no more violence," Aulus interrupted.

Antedios fell silent, his mouth tightening as Aulus signaled to his soldiers. They swarmed through the village like ants as they entered the homes that surrounded the square. The villagers cried out in dissent, looking at Antedios. But he gestured for everyone to stand-down.

Hot anger flowed through Boudica. What right did these Roman soldiers have to come into their homes, to take their weapons? The warrior class was the most important in the tribe; their weapons were as necessary to them as any limb. Boudica had a small dagger tucked beneath her bed, one that Prasutagus had procured for her; she'd thankfully hidden the rest of her weapons in the same forest clearing where she practiced.

"Step back," Rozen said, grabbing Boudica and Kensa and forcing them against the wall as two soldiers approached their home. Her voice wavered with fear; Boudica had rarely seen Rozen display such trepidation.

Her heart pounded against her chest as the two soldiers entered. Boudica had to bite her lip not to cry out as the soldiers tossed aside their beds of animal furs. One found her hidden dagger, picking it up with a sneer.

The second soldier knocked down the loom that Rozen had just been weaving on and kicked aside the animal pelts they used for sitting whenever Rozen told them stories, shattered the clay pots and baskets in the storage area; they even tore down the slabs of salted meats hanging from the rafters in the far corner.

The first soldier moved to Rozen's bed of furs,

tossing it aside to reveal a fine iron sword. Boudica stifled a gasp. She didn't know Rozen had a weapon; she thought Rozen hated weapons.

Rozen's eyes went wild, and she stepped forward, holding out her hands in a beseeching gesture.

"Please, it's an heirloom. It belonged to my husband; he's now with the gods."

But the soldiers ignored her, holding onto the sword, along with Boudica's dagger.

"Please—" Rozen begged, her voice breaking on a sob. She grasped the tunic of one of the soldiers, but he turned and struck her in the abdomen with the butt of his sword.

Boudica darted forward as Rozen crumbled to the ground, helping her up. A wave of fury swept over her, and she glared at the soldiers.

"You have what you came for," Boudica hissed. "Leave."

The soldier's mouth tightened. His body was broad and muscular, but he had a narrow face that reminded her of a snake's. He stalked toward her with deadly purpose, unsheathing his sword.

"No!" Rozen protested, straightening, even as she winced with pain. "Please, she—"

"Shut up," the soldier barked. He reached out to grab Boudica by her hair, yanking her toward him. His eyes ran up and down her body, and icy dread coiled around her.

"Please!" Rozen's voice behind her wavered with fear. "Please leave her be. She is just a child!"

The soldier ignored Rozen, his dark eyes pinned on Boudica's face. Boudica tried not to let her fear show, tried to let only defiance shine in her eyes, but she recalled the other whispers she'd overheard about Roman soldiers, whispers about what they did to the women of the tribes they conquered, and she trembled in the soldier's grasp.

The soldier leaned in toward her, his lips close to her ear. Revulsion rose in her throat like a bitter ale, and she suppressed a wave of nausea.

"I wonder what a barbarian cunt feels like," he whispered.

Behind her, Rozen and Kensa began to beg and weep. Boudica closed her eyes, the hot sting of tears burning her lids. *Please,* she prayed to the gods. *Spare me.*

"You have retrieved the weapons from this home. Remove your hands from my daughter and leave now."

Her father's voice, firm and commanding, splintered the tense silence. Boudica's eyes flew open as the soldier released her.

Boudica stumbled back, and Rozen pulled her into her arms. Looking past Rozen's shoulder, she saw Antedios standing in the doorway, flanked by Judoc and Prasutagus. Fury tightened both his and Prasutagus's faces, and Judoc had his hand on Prasutagus's arm, restraining him.

The soldiers turned to face Antedios. For several moments they said nothing, and the threat of violence hung in the air. Boudica's shoulders sank with relief as the two soldiers finally left Rozen's home without a word.

Antedios and Prasutagus both lingered in the doorway, their eyes trained on Boudica. Concern filled Prasutagus's expression, while Antedios's eyes remained unreadable.

"We're fine, Chieftain Antedios," Rozen said, still holding Boudica in her arms. "Thank you."

It was only when they left that Boudica allowed her tears to fall, weeping into Rozen's shoulder as she stroked her hair. Kensa moved to her side, whispering words of comfort. Boudica hated her weakness; she should have taken the soldier's sword and stabbed him straight through.

If a Roman soldier attacks me again, she silently vowed, as her tears subsided, *I will not weep. I will not cower. I will fight.*

THE VILLAGERS REMAINED TENSE EVEN AFTER the Romans left, and the farmers returned to their fields, the craftsmen to their shops, the women to their embroidery and cooking. Rozen remained silent, her face pale, and when she thought Boudica and Kensa weren't looking, Boudica saw tears glisten in her eyes. She'd never known how much Rozen had missed her deceased husband until now, and remnant fury went through her at the callousness of the

Roman soldiers. Had Boudica known the sword was there and that it meant so much to Rozen, she would have taken and hidden it with her other weapons. She would have tried to stop the Romans from taking the sword. Instead, she'd frozen and wept like a coward.

After their midday meal, Rozen told them she was going to fetch wool from a neighbor, but Boudica saw Rozen make her way to the edge of the village, to the home of Mael.

"She's going to seek blessings for her husband," Kensa said, joining Boudica at the doorway.

"I didn't know she had her husband's sword," Boudica said. "I should have stopped them."

"If your father couldn't stop them, how could you?" Kensa asked. "Rozen used to say the gods will punish the Romans. That someone will one day challenge their power."

Boudica considered Kensa's words, wondering if it would ever be possible to challenge the Roman army, the ravenous wolves who commanded armies with such strength that her mighty father had bent the knee to avoid their wrath.

She heard a chorus of male cries and turned, noticing several male nobles entering Antedios's home. Boudica stilled. What were her father and the nobles discussing? Were they planning to challenge the Romans? To get back their weapons?

"Where are you going? We haven't finished our

embroidery," Kensa said, frowning as Boudica stepped out of the home.

"I'll be back," Boudica said shortly. She turned and ducked her head low, trying to keep out of sight as she approached her father's home. Women, unless they were warriors, were not permitted at the meetings Antedios held; she must not be seen.

Boudica made her way to the rear of Antedios's home, pressing herself close to the door but keeping out of sight.

"Get them out of that cowardly armor and put them up against any of our warriors . . . we'd kill them with our bare hands!" one noble cried.

"Can we reason with them?" It was Prasutagus's voice, heavy with caution. "The governor has usually been fair with us."

"He's still one of them," Mael returned gruffly. "He still took our weapons. I never wanted our tribe to ally with the Romans. They can't be trusted. Their soldiers threatened your own daughter. We can't stand for this."

Boudica held her breath as the men fell silent, waiting for Antedios's reply.

"Aye, they did threaten my daughter," he said finally, his voice thick with rage. "And a man's weapons . . . they're a part of who he is. His honor. His manhood. They seek to take this away?"

His powerful voice rose with anger, and he spoke two simple words.

"We fight."

The nobles shouted their agreement; many bellowed tribal battle cries. Boudica smiled, relief coursing through her.

But disappointment immediately struck her; Antedios wouldn't allow her to join the fight. *And why would he?* she thought with a stab of shame. Antedios had beaten her in the combat challenge and she'd frozen when that soldier attacked her.

"We gather anything we can use for weapons—any weapons we managed to hide from their soldiers. Then we march west to the nearest Roman fort in two days' time after we prepare. Feast, rest, bed your wives. You will all need your strength," Antedios continued.

She heard the nobles filing out and made her way toward the entrance. Antedios might not allow her to fight, but she could help in her own way. He needed to know about the stash of weapons she had hidden in the forest, even if he would scold her for it.

She stepped inside. Only Antedios and Mael remained, their heads close together as they spoke in hushed tones. Antedios looked up, and she braced herself for his usual dismissal. But he gestured for her to come forward.

"I was about to have an attendant come fetch you. Mael, leave us. There's something I wish to discuss with my daughter alone."

Surprise skittered through her. Antedios rarely sent for her. A rush of hope swirled through her chest. Perhaps he needed all the bodies he could get, and he would allow her to fight? Perhaps he would allow her to personally exact her revenge on that Roman soldier? Unable to stop the smile of hope that curved her lips, she approached Antedios as Mael left them alone.

"Are you . . . unharmed?" Antedios asked, his gaze sweeping over her face with concern.

Boudica stilled. This wasn't the same man who'd pressed his foot to her throat with fire in his eyes. When she didn't answer right away, he continued, "You seemed frightened. I wanted to cut out the insides of those soldiers with my sword."

"I shouldn't have been frightened," Boudica said, another wave of shame washing over her as she recalled the way she'd wept in Rozen's arms like a child. What type of warrior wept after facing an enemy? "I should have fought off that soldier."

"And then you would be dead," Antedios said, his tone flat. The softness had gone from his voice, replaced by the admonishment she was used to hearing from him. "Sometimes it's wise to be fearful and cautious, to not give in to the heat of your rage."

"Is that why you allowed them to take our weapons?" she asked, her defiance and anger boiling to the surface.

Antedios's eyes widened at her boldness, and she waited for his scolding words. But he surprised her again.

"If I hadn't . . . there would've been slaughter," Antedios replied, after a brief pause. "We weren't prepared to fight." His eyes darkened, a shadow flaring in their depths. "It's happened before."

"We still have some weapons," Boudica said, swallowing. "I—I know you forbid it, but I have weapons hidden in the forest. The warriors can use them against the Romans."

And me, she silently added. *I can help in the fight. Let me prove how strong I can be.*

"I know about your weapons," Antedios said, and Boudica tensed. "I knew if the Romans were ever to do something like this . . . it would help to have your hidden stores. We also have weapons hidden in two other sites in the forest."

Boudica's surprise faded, replaced by pride. Perhaps Antedios was one step ahead of the Romans. Perhaps he would defeat them and even purge the Romans from their lands.

"I've asked you here to inform you I've chosen your betrothed," Antedios continued. "I was to tell you earlier today, but after the Romans arrived . . ." He trailed off, shaking his head. "I hoped to have more time to prepare you. But it's best that you're wed before battle for matters of inheritance."

Wed? She knew her father would want her to wed at some point in the months to come; she hadn't expected it to be so soon. Shock and fury careened through Boudica; she clenched her fists at her sides. She kept her gaze trained on the ground so her father wouldn't see the anger in her eyes.

"I understand," she forced herself to say, trying to keep her voice steady. "Who am I to wed?"

"Prasutagus," he said, as she raised stunned eyes to meet his.

Boudica's throat went dry, another emotion she couldn't identify racing through her. Antedios's eyes remained on her, watching her carefully, as if waiting for the storm inside her to erupt.

But she knew she had no choice. Her protests would be met by Antedios's stern insistence. Girls left the homes of the families who fostered them and went right to their husband's home. She was the chieftain's daughter; it was her duty.

"Thank you for telling me, Father," she whispered. She saw the surprise in his eyes, the wariness that slowly dissipated. He'd expected her to protest, to fight, to plead. But if she was to be a warrior one day, she needed to prove she could take orders. That she could do her duty. "I'll start preparing."

With her shoulders straight, her arms stiff at her sides, she turned to leave Antedios's home, ignoring the growing storm that brewed inside her.

4

Once Boudica's anger had subsided, a cold bitterness took its place. She wondered if Prasutagus knew of her father's plans. He was close to Antedios, as close as any father and son. She recalled the look Prasutagus had given her in the clearing after their sword fight, and then by the stream when he comforted her after the ritual feast. Had there been desire in his gaze? Had Prasutagus been the one to choose her? Or was he making himself desire her, in the way that husbands desired wives, knowing that he too had no choice?

She wasn't able to confront him. The next day, he and the other warriors retreated to the forests from first light until night to prepare for the upcoming battle. She realized with a heavy feeling in her chest that she likely wouldn't see him until the ceremony

"You should be happy," Kensa said the night before the ceremony, as they sat cross-legged on animal pelts before the hearth's fire. They each sipped jugs of ale, but the liquid had no taste for Boudica as she stared listlessly into the flames.

"Why?" Boudica asked, frowning at Kensa. "I've no desire to be a wife. Father knows this, as does Prasutagus."

"Because Prasutagus is young, handsome, and you already care for each other. Many brides barely know their husbands before they're wed. And everyone knows he'll be chieftain someday; your father loves him. You'll be the most powerful woman in the tribe."

But not in the way I want, Boudica thought, frustration roiling through her.

Rozen entered with a basket of warm bread, frowning with disapproval when she saw that Kensa and Boudica were still awake.

"You must rest, child," Rozen scolded Boudica, gesturing to her bed of furs. "Tomorrow is an important day."

Boudica's mouth tightened, but she obeyed, crawling into bed. Boudica's pending ceremony had pulled Rozen out of her sadness over the Romans taking her husband's sword; she'd thrown herself into preparations with merriment. Boudica had tried to hide her resentment from Rozen; she wanted her foster mother's happiness, even if she dreaded becoming a wife.

Boudica turned to face the wall, closing her eyes as Rozen cheerfully hummed in the far corner. If she strained her ears, she could hear the distant rumble of male voices from her father's home. The nobles met each night to discuss the upcoming battle.

What's their strategy? Boudica wondered. *Will they take the Romans by surprise? Will they join with other tribes for greater numbers? If they succeed, will the Romans leave us be? Or will they retaliate?*

She fell asleep with worried, racing thoughts, and awoke at first light, blinking at the sight of several noblewomen and attendants milling around the home, along with Rozen and Kensa.

Rozen met her eyes as Boudica sat up. She crossed the room and knelt by her bed, taking her hands.

"I didn't want to wake you yet; I know you need your rest for today. Oh, child," she continued with a sigh. "I know you're not happy to be wed. But your life will not be a quiet one. The gods have plans for you. I feel it in my bones."

Rozen reached up to dab at her eyes with the hem of her tunic, and a rush of emotion filled Boudica. She'd been so consumed by anger over her impending marriage, it hadn't struck her until now that she would leave the home she'd grown up in—and the only mother she'd ever known. Tears sprang to her eyes, and she reached out to embrace Rozen.

"The gods didn't deem me worthy of having children of my own," Rozen murmured, returning Boudica's embrace, stroking her hair. "But you and Kensa are like my very own. Will you still come see me after you're wed?"

"I will," Boudica said, pulling back as she blinked away her tears. "I promise."

Rozen smiled, reaching up to cup the side of Boudica's face, before her expression turned stern.

"All right, child," Rozen said, her voice wavering, "it's time to get you prepared."

An attendant brought in a wooden bath and helped Boudica bathe. Afterward, the attendant anointed her body with oil, then with rosemary and lavender. Kensa and another attendant helped her dress in a blue silk tunic embroidered with gold stitching. The attendant placed a golden torc around her arm, while Kensa fastened a golden armlet to her other arm as the attendant braided her hair into a long plait, winding it at the base of her nape with a golden comb. Rozen darkened her brows with blackberries and reddened her cheeks with berries from nearby alder trees.

When they'd finished preparing her, Rozen stepped back, her eyes glistening with tears. She reached out to give Boudica a bronze-backed hand mirror.

Boudica took it, studying her reflection with surprise. The face of a stranger stared back at her. She looked like one of the noblewomen of the tribe when they came to one of her father's feasts in all of their finery.

Defiance welled deep within her; she didn't want

to be here, preparing to wed. She wanted to be with the warriors, preparing to fight.

Duty, she reminded herself. *Every warrior must do their duty.*

She looked up at Rozen and forced a smile.

"I'm ready," she said.

Rozen, Kensa, and Boudica's attendants trailed her from the home, making their way to the forest. She was to wed in the same sacred grove where the druids performed their ceremonies to please the gods. It was where all nobles wed, and where her father had wed her mother.

Dozens of nobles had gathered in the grove and turned to face them as they approached. Antedios stood next to Mael, who was dressed in white ceremonial robes. Raw emotion flared in Antedios's eyes at the sight of Boudica in her wedding finery, but it vanished before she could discern its meaning, his expression returning to a stoic mask.

Boudica turned to face Prasutagus, who stood next to Mael and Antedios. She thought her anger and resentment would flare at the sight of him; instead, a fierce heat spread throughout her body. He stood towering in the center of the grove in a fine green tunic, the sunlight highlighting his handsome features, his amber eyes intent on hers.

Color stained her cheeks, and she lowered her

gaze as she stepped forward. *I'm doing my duty,* she told herself, ignoring the awareness that spiraled through her as Prasutagus took both her hands in his, and Mael bound their hands together with embroidered fabric, chanting the words of a wedding prayer.

When he concluded the prayer, she finally looked up at Prasutagus, and started at the raw longing and desire in his eyes.

Boudica tore her eyes away as Antedios announced they were to all dine in his home for a celebratory feast. Prasutagus kept her hand in his as they trailed the guests to Antedios's home, where they sat at the head of the home next to her father as the guests of honor, while attendants served them a meal of smoked fish, roasted pork, wine, and bread.

As everyone dined, Antedios moved to the center of the home, gesturing for silence as he turned to face Boudica and Prasutagus, raising his cup of wine.

"May the gods bless you with many sons."

Boudica forced a smile as the guests cheered and let out raucous cries of agreement. She felt Prasutagus's burning gaze on her flushed face, but she kept her focus on her food.

Unease coiled around her at the thought of what lay ahead. She'd given little thought to her wedding night, but now she recalled the whispered gossip she'd overheard from married women in the tribe. They spoke of a brief pain they felt the moment their husbands made them women, and the bleeding between their thighs. At the thought, another wave of resentment swept over her. The only way she wanted a man to make her bleed was on the battlefield.

The raucous cries of the warriors around her forced her thoughts back to the present. She looked up; several warriors stood around her father, boasting of the Romans they would kill during the next day's battle. Despite their boasting, she could hear anxiety in their voices. *Their boasting is a shield*, she realized. They feared the battle to come.

Dread filled her, and she looked at her father. At the moment, he seemed powerful and strong, standing in the center of his home, but even he had bowed down to the Romans once. What if they defeated him in battle? She'd heard rumors of the Romans great numbers, how they could fight as one—even when there were many of them.

She slid a glance at Prasutagus, who was no longer focused on her, his gaze lowered as he sipped his wine. While she didn't want to be married to Prasutagus, she cared for him and didn't want him to come to harm in battle. He was a fine fighter, and her father was even better, but unease now replaced her envy at the thought of them fighting the Romans, an unease which remained throughout the feast and to its conclusion, when she and Prasutagus were escorted to their new marital home by Antedios, Mael, Rozen and Kensa.

Their new home had once belonged to Prasutagus's father; it was even larger than Rozen's, standing on the edge of the village square. Attendants had already lit the hearth in the center of the home, and a large bed of animal furs lay before it. The home was otherwise empty; it was up to Boudica and her new attendants to fill it with belongings and make it into a true home.

Antedios, Rozen, and Kensa remained by the doorway as Prasutagus and Boudica trailed Mael inside. They knelt before the hearth as he blessed them, praying to the gods for Boudica to bear strong sons who'd one day fight for and lead their tribe. He then left them alone with a respectful bow.

Boudica turned, watching them go. Kensa glanced back at her and gave her a sly smile; Boudica quickly looked away. She knew the reason for Kensa's sly smile; tonight she was to become a woman and lie with her new husband.

Boudica swallowed, her heart hammering in her chest as she gazed into the flames of the fire. This wasn't sparring or a combat challenge; she wasn't certain of what she was supposed to do. Keeping her gaze lowered, she started to lift her tunic. But Prasutagus placed a restraining hand on her arm.

She looked up at him, startled.

"We—we're to lie together," she said, past dry lips. "It's our duty."

"Yes," Prasutagus said gently. "But we don't have to tonight. Look at you. You're shaking like a leaf. I won't bed my wife when she can't even look at me."

Wife. The word seared into Boudica like a cast-iron brand. She closed her eyes, dropping her hands to her sides and getting to her feet, her anger returning.

"How long have you known about our betrothal? Why didn't you tell me?" she demanded.

"Your father told me the day before the Beltane festival. I wanted to tell you during our sword fight, but he insisted I hold my tongue."

"You know I never wanted to wed, Prasutagus. You could have told him; he listens to you. I want—"

"To be a warrior. I know. But your father will never allow it—you're his only living heir. I hoped—" Prasutagus faltered, searching her eyes, some foreign emotion in his eyes that Boudica didn't recognize. "I hoped you cared for me. The way I care for you."

"I—I do care for you," she whispered. "Besides Kensa, you're the only friend I have. But I never wanted to be a wife. I'm doing this because it's my duty."

"Well, we are wed now, as the chieftain wished," Prasutagus said, turning away from her, his mouth tightening. "If you never wish to lie with me, I'll never force you. I won't say anything to Antedios if that's your choice. After a time . . . your father will allow me to take a second wife."

A sudden and surprising sliver of jealousy snaked through her at the thought. Boudica expelled a breath, reaching out to take his hand.

"Give me some time to get used to this," she whispered. "Please."

Prasutagus's eyes softened, and he raised her

hand to his lips, kissing it. That familiar heat roiled through her at the feel of his lips on her skin.

"All right," he agreed.

Moments later, they lay on their bed of animal furs, still clothed, facing each other.

"I remember when I first saw you," Prasutagus murmured, giving her a gentle smile. "You were still a girl, practicing your embroidery with Rozen and Kensa. I could see in your eyes how much you hated it. But your eyes lit up when you watched me and the other boys train with daggers and swords. I'd never seen such longing on a young girl's face."

Boudica smiled; she remembered that moment well. She'd been in her ninth year, and she'd snuck away from Rozen's home to watch the boys fight in the fields that lay just beyond the village. Prasutagus had met her eyes, a look of amusement filling his as he noticed her hiding behind a roundhouse as she watched the boys fight. She'd fled back to Rozen's home, terrified that he'd tell Rozen or her father that she'd snuck away from her duties. But he'd said nothing. Days later, he gave her his sword to practice with in private, away from Rozen's prying eyes.

"You gave me your sword," Boudica said, her smile widening at the memory. "It was the best gift I'd ever received."

"I knew the sword would mean more to you. I've never loved fighting as much as you."

"But you're a member of the warrior class," Boudica said, disbelief sweeping over her. "And you're a fine fighter. One of the best in the tribe. You helped train me."

"It was the only way I could be alone with you," Prasutagus admitted. Surprise coursed through her as he continued, "I hoped that one day you would look at me with the same longing with which you looked at the sword. I've always just wanted to tend to the lands, but my father was a warrior, and it was his wish that I follow the same path."

He reached out to touch the side of her face, and she found herself leaning in to his touch.

"Sleep, now," he murmured. "Wife."

Wife. The term didn't sting as much as it had before. She reached up to grip his hand.

"Be careful during the battle tomorrow. Please."

"You care if your husband lives?"

"Of course," she breathed, a sharp sting of grief piercing her at the thought of his death. "I care for you. Promise me you'll fight well tomorrow."

"I will," Prasutagus said. "Now sleep, wife. All will be well."

But Boudica's dread had returned, and it followed her into her anxious dreams, like a ruthless beast determined to devour its prey.

5

Boudica awoke to the sound of battle cries; a familiar sound the morning of a battle when the warriors worked themselves into a frenzy before marching.

Prasutagus was already awake, standing in the far corner of their home, dressed in a loose tunic and braccae, while an attendant hovered before him, painting tribal tattoos onto both of his arms.

"Leave us," she told the attendant as she got to her feet and approached. She took the small jug of war paint from the attendant, waiting until she left before addressing him.

"Why didn't you wake me?"

"There was no need."

"Yes, there is. I want to see you off," Boudica said, hurt prickling at her chest. "I'm—I'm your wife. I can help you get prepared for battle."

"But you don't wish to be my wife," Prasutagus

said, studying her closely. "And wives don't prepare their husbands for battle."

"This wife will," Boudica said, choosing to disregard his statement about not wanting to be his wife. She dipped her finger into the jug of green warpaint and applied it to Prasutagus's arm, continuing the work the attendant had begun. "If I can't go to battle, I'll at least help you prepare."

Prasutagus stood still as she adorned his body with the intricate tattoos of their tribe in silence. She'd watched attendants prepare warriors for battle since she was a girl and had memorized every step, from the intricate tribal tattoos that warded off death and evil spirits, to the careful washing of the hair with lime, arranging each strand of hair until they were spiked and shaped like a horse's mane.

The heat of Prasutagus's gaze on her face seared her skin the entire time, but she didn't look up at him until she was done, stepping back. Though his tribal tattoos and spiked hair gave him the fierce appearance of a warrior, she could only see the gentle and kind friend she'd grown up with. Her husband.

She looked down, noticing that her hands shook, the heavy realization that he was about to march into battle with the treacherous Romans settling over her. Prasutagus took in her shaking hands with a concerned frown.

"The Romans. . . they've only a small unit," he said gently. "We can handle them."

Boudica met his eyes and nodded, though her

unease from the night before had returned, filling her with a dark foreboding. He reached out to take her shaking hands in his, and rather than resist the warmth that rushed through her at his touch, she relished it.

He released her hands, and she changed into a fresh tunic before she and Prasutagus left, making their way out to the central square.

An army of the tribe's warriors had gathered there, many shouting tribal cries, their voices ringing out over the square. It was customary for the rest of the tribe to trail the warriors to the battlefield and watch the fight. But this was a surprise attack, they couldn't risk alerting the Romans of their presence.

Through the sea of men, Boudica saw Kensa embrace Arthek, the young man she wished to marry. Arthek cupped the sides of Kensa's face, leaning down to kiss her.

Boudica flushed, turning to look up at Prasutagus. Would he kiss her as well?

Prasutagus reached out to pull her into his arms, holding her close for a moment, so close that she could hear his heartbeat thundering along with her own. Anticipation hung in their silence, but Prasutagus released her, giving her a brief nod before turning to disappear into the crowd of men.

Disappointment roiled through her. She shook her head, telling herself that she didn't want Prasutagus to kiss her. She just wanted him to return, safe and unharmed.

Come back alive, she told him silently, watching his dark head vanish into the crowd. *Andraste, please watch over him.*

"Prasutagus may have a gentle heart, but he's a fierce warrior," Rozen murmured from behind her.

Boudica turned. She'd not heard her foster mother approach. Rozen gave her a kind smile, taking her hand and pulling her into the crook of her arm. Grateful for Rozen's presence, Boudica rested her head on her shoulder.

They stood in silence for a moment before Rozen spoke again. "Your father wishes to see you before the men depart. He's in his home."

Boudica straightened, giving Rozen a puzzled frown. What could her father want? She'd done her duty and married the man he'd chosen for her.

When she arrived in Antedios's home, several guards and advisors surrounded him. He was dressed for battle; unlike Prasutagus, who wore his tunic, her father was shirtless, his broad chest covered with tribal tattoos, his gold chieftain's torc on his arm, his red hair spiked back into a mane; he reminded Boudica of a fierce horse come to life.

Antedios turned as she entered, waving away his guards. He gestured for her to come forward and took her hand, placing a brooch in her palm. She looked down; it was a golden brooch in the shape of a horse.

"It belonged to your mother," he said gruffly. "I gave it to her after we were betrothed. She loved horses . . . loved riding. I see her spirit in you."

It was the first time Antedios had ever spoken of her mother. Rozen had told her she'd been his favorite wife; he mourned her for years after she joined the gods. Boudica had scant memories of her mother, other than her kind smile and the low hum of her voice whenever she sang a young Boudica to sleep.

Boudica clutched the brooch in her hand, the only tangible connection to her mother, and a rush of emotion filled her chest.

"Thank you, Father."

Boudica met her father's steady gaze, wondering with a stab of dread if this was the last time she'd see him. She struggled for words; he wasn't one for sentiment. She needed to keep her words simple, though there was much she wanted to say.

I hope you'll one day see me as worthy of becoming a warrior, of being your heir. I want to make you proud. I know I can. I love you.

But she said none of those things.

"I'll—I'll pray to the gods for your victory," she whispered instead.

Antedios's gaze lingered on hers, as if he sensed there was more she wanted to say. Boudica waited for his response, but the silence stretched, and Antedios looked away. A stab of hurt pierced her as he dismissed her with a wave, turning to issue orders to his guards.

After the army departed from the main square, accompanied by clappers and the tribal cries of the warriors, Boudica invited Kensa and Rozen to her home for a midday meal. She didn't wish to eat alone with her worried thoughts consuming her.

When they arrived, Boudica noticed that Kensa was quiet, her mouth tight and her brow furrowed with worry for Arthek. Rozen made great effort to fill the silence with cheerful chatter, speaking of Boudica and Prasutagus's ceremony and how lovely it was.

"I prayed to the goddess Damara for you to have strong sons," Rozen gushed, and a sudden stab of regret pierced Boudica. If Prasutagus died on the battlefield, he would have no heir because she hadn't lain with him.

She forced away the thought. Prasutagus wouldn't die on the battlefield. *He'll come back,* she told herself. *He will return.*

After the meal, Rozen left after giving Boudica a long embrace, but Kensa lingered behind. She reached out to squeeze Boudica's hand.

"I know you never wished to wed," she murmured. "But I can see how frightened you are about the battle. You can admit to yourself that you love him. It will make your life with him easier—and happier."

Kensa released her hand and left before Boudica could protest. She swallowed, refusing to mull over Kensa's words, to take them to heart.

Looking down at the brooch her father had given

her, she touched its intricate design, worry gripping her heart. She wished she had the gift of foresight, to know the outcome of the battle, to know if her father and husband would return home alive.

Boudica stilled as a thought seized her. She didn't have the sight, but it was rumored that Mael did.

She hurried out of her home, heading toward Mael's home on the far edge of the square, the second largest home in the village after her father's. But she saw him and several other druid priests leave his home and head into the forest, dressed in their white ceremonial robes.

She hesitated, but only for a moment, before following them, taking care to maintain her distance. It was forbidden to watch or interrupt the priests as they carried out rituals without their knowledge; the priests' communion with the gods was sacred. But what Boudica needed from Mael could not wait.

She trailed Mael and the priests to a grove deep in the forest, taking refuge behind a large oak tree.

One priest had a hare in its grip, and Mael took it from him, moving with it to the center of the grove where he dragged his knife across the animal's throat. He placed the dying hare on the ground, and the priests knelt around it. Mael remained standing, closing his eyes as he uttered a prayer to the gods. The gods communicated to the priests through sacrifice, and Boudica watched anxiously as Mael studied the dying hare.

Mael abruptly tensed, his gaze landing on the tree she sat crouched behind.

"Come forward, child."

Shock rendered her still. How did he know?

"Child," he repeated. "Come forward."

Shaking, Boudica clambered to her feet and stepped out from behind the tree. The other priests turned, scowling in disapproval at the sight of her.

"I wasn't going to interrupt," she said hastily. "I only wish to—"

"You fear for your husband and your father," Mael interrupted, his gaze steady on hers.

"Yes," Boudica said, blinking back a wave of tears. "I want you to perform a divination. I want to know if they'll survive the battle."

The priests murmured words of disapproval, but Mael remained silent as he studied her, his black eyes unreadable. After a long moment, he turned to face the priests.

"Leave me alone with the child."

The priests froze. One looked as if he might protest, but at the sharp look in Mael's eyes, they obeyed, leaving Boudica and Mael alone.

"Stand back, child."

Boudica obeyed, taking several steps back as Mael's gaze lowered to the animal, who now lay dead.

Mael closed his eyes and whispered another prayer. He began to tremble as he whispered, before lurching forward, taking her arms in a firm grip. His eyes opened to focus on her, but they were pools of white, blank and unseeing.

"I see . . . death," Mael said. His voice was strained; he spoke barely above a whisper. "I see . . . life. Fire . . . blood. It pours from the skies."

His eyes cleared and returned to their normal shade of dark umber. He blinked, gazing at her as if seeing her for the first time.

"I see . . . your face, Boudica."

Mael's hands dropped to his sides, and he stepped back.

"You saw me?" she breathed. "What does that mean? What of the battle? Will my father or Prasutagus—"

"I've seen what the gods have chosen to show me, child. Nothing more."

I SEE YOUR FACE, BOUDICA.

Mael's words haunted her for the rest of the day. Did that mean she would still become a great warrior someday? Or did it mean something darker? She recalled his words with a chill. *I see . . . fire . . . blood.*

Night soon fell, casting the village in darkness. Boudica crawled into the bed of animal furs she and Prasutagus had shared the night before, her heart racing as she listened to the crackling of the fire in the hearth, trying to quell her worried thoughts.

When fatigue claimed her, and she was on the

verge of sleep, she heard frantic voices outside her home. The army had returned.

Boudica scrambled out of bed, tugging her cloak around her, and made her way to the central square.

She froze as she saw the warriors stream back into the village, dread filling her heart. When there was a victory, the warriors returned to the village amid a barrage of triumphant tribal cries, with heads of their enemies slung from the necks of their horses or carried aloft.

There were no signs of triumph now; the warriors were all silent and grim. Many pulled bodies of the dead behind them in wagons and chariots.

Fear tightened her chest and Boudica pushed through the crowd searching for Prasutagus and Antedios. *Please,* she prayed to Andraste. *Please let them be alive.*

She spotted Prasutagus at the rear of the army, limping and supported by two men, but alive. Tears of relief stung her eyes, and she rushed forward. The men stepped aside as they embraced. Boudica pulled back, searching his face.

"My father . . . ?"

Prasutagus said nothing. Raw grief flared in his eyes, and the dread that had settled in the pit of her stomach expanded. She looked past Prasutagus's broad shoulders, and her mouth went dry.

Antedios's guards pulled a chariot toward the square. Inside lay her father's still body.

Boudica stood frozen, shock and disbelief

coursing through her. Chieftain Antedios . . . dead? Defeated?

She shook her head. It wasn't possible. That still form in the chariot couldn't be her father. She stumbled forward, approaching it. His guards stopped, averting their eyes as Boudica gazed down at the man inside.

It was indeed Antedios. There was the red hair she shared, the prominent brow, the strong jaw. The man who'd swung her up into his arms when she was a girl, who'd whispered words of love to her when he thought she couldn't hear. The man who'd scolded her for wanting to fight, because she was his only heir, his child, his beloved. The man she'd one day hoped to make proud by standing at his side on the battlefield. The man she'd loved with every part of her, who'd been torn from this life. From her.

A chasm of despair opened up inside her, and she let out a grief-stricken wail.

6

Boudica stood with the mourners at the edge of her father's burial pit, as the priests murmured their prayers and left offerings to accompany him on his journey to the gods. They'd buried him in his finest clothes, and a golden torc adorned his neck while another encircled his arm. He lay in the center of a royal wagon in the burial pit, which his attendants had filled with his favorite food and drink; mutton, salted pork, mead and ale, along with his finest drinking cups and a bronze cauldron.

She watched as his attendants removed the wheels from the wagon, lowering it to the ground and propping the wheels against the side of the pit. They climbed out, and the warriors of the tribe stepped forward to cover the pit with dirt while Mael uttered a final prayer.

It wasn't until her father's body disappeared beneath the dirt the warriors cast over him that her grief rose, fierce and intense, tightening around her throat like a noose, robbing her of air. As the chieftain's daughter, his only living heir, she was expected to display strength, but it took great effort to hold herself still, to not allow her legs to give way beneath the onslaught of her anguish.

When the prayers concluded, and the mourners filed away, she remained frozen, gazing down at the earth where her father was buried.

Behind her, she heard Prasutagus whisper to Rozen and Kensa, and their footfalls as they walked away. Prasutagus approached, stopping at her side.

"When your father came to me about wedding you, he told me how strong you were after your mother's death, how you wouldn't allow yourself to cry even though you were just a child. He said . . . 'My daughter will always do her best not to cry, not to show her pain. But everyone, even the strongest warrior, has pain.'" He paused, allowing his words to settle before he continued. "Antedios told me that my duty as your husband was to allow you to show your pain, to never shield any emotion you think is a weakness."

Boudica stilled, shock and surprise filling her. She'd always thought her father barely noticed her, but he'd noticed how she tried to hide any weakness from him, from the tribe. Her father may have known her more than she realized.

Tears sprang to her eyes, but she didn't blink them away. Prasutagus reached out and pulled her into the warmth of his arms. They stood there, still and silent, until Boudica allowed Prasutagus to lead her away.

Her sleep was restless and filled with images of her father's lifeless body, and she awoke several times, only to have Prasutagus pull her into his arms, allowing her to weep against his chest.

She came to just after first light. Prasutagus was still asleep, his arms splayed wide above his head. She took in the dark fringe of his lashes, his slightly parted lips. And beneath her lingering grief, tenderness stirred. He shifted, his eyes fluttering open to meet hers. He reached up to touch the side of her face, and she leaned in to his touch, allowing the warmth to spread through her, to quell the pull of her grief.

An attendant entered, and Boudica pulled back from him, a flush spreading across her face.

"The nobles wish to see you in the chieftain's home," the attendant told Prasutagus, giving them both a respectful bow.

Boudica's heart picked up its pace; she knew what this meant. Antedios had wanted Prasutagus to succeed him as chieftain.

Prasutagus gave the attendant a nod, but he looked at her with concern; he looked reluctant to leave her.

"Go," Boudica whispered, reaching out to touch his hand. "I'll be fine."

Prasutagus returned just after she finished her morning meal, his face flushed as he approached her.

"They're making me chieftain," he said, his eyes a storm of conflict.

Boudica stilled. It was confirmation that her father was truly gone. But if anyone should be chieftain, it was Prasutagus. He was a fierce fighter; kind, loyal, and well-liked. She stepped forward, taking his hands, and the tumult in his eyes calmed.

"My father would be proud."

As the sun descended beneath the distant horizon, Boudica stood with the nobles in her father's former home while Mael blessed Prasutagus, placing one of her father's golden torcs around his neck and proclaiming him chieftain of the tribe.

As he stood, the nobles shouted triumphant tribal cries. He met her eyes, and Boudica smiled.

Yet the celebratory feast was somber. During such feasts, Antedios's voice dominated the home as he requested tales from the bards or demanded to see combat challenges from the warriors. Prasutagus was a quieter presence; he spoke in low tones to Mael, who sat at his side, while the other nobles drank and feasted around them. Boudica maintained her forced smile throughout the feast, trying to set aside the many memories she had of her father in this home, presiding over ritual feasts, his laughter echoing off the walls.

Their attendants moved them into Antedios's

home that same night. Boudica stood in the center while servants arranged her and Prasutagus's bed of animal furs in the far corner where her father once slept. She wondered if this would always feel like her father's home, his presence lingering like the persistent scent of wood smoke.

When their attendants left them alone, Boudica moved to the hearth. She sat cross-legged before it, reaching out to warm her fingers.

"We'd no chance. The Romans knew we were coming."

Boudica turned to look at Prasutagus. He stood by the doorway, looking past her at the flames. It was the first he'd spoken of the battle that killed Antedios. There was a part of her that wanted him to not speak of it, not when her grief was still raw. But there was another part, a stronger part, that needed to know how Antedios, a strong warrior, had been defeated.

"The Romans fought together, almost as one. It was not a quick battle as we hoped. I thought Antedios would call for a retreat. But he fought until the end. The Romans knew he was our leader; they surrounded him. I think they wanted to capture him, perhaps to take him back to Rome in chains. Your father would never allow them to take him. He fought all until he could fight no more. We had no choice but to retreat; it was by the gods' grace we were able to retrieve his body."

Boudica closed her eyes, tears stinging her lids at the thought of her father's final stand against the

Romans. She could see him in her mind's eye, letting out a ferocious cry as he leaped toward them with his sword outstretched, toward his inevitable death.

"If those other tribes hadn't rebelled, they'd never have come for our weapons. None of this would have happened," Prasutagus continued, his voice trembling with anger.

Boudica's eyes flew open with astonishment. She stumbled to her feet, glaring at him.

"Those tribes fought for their homeland. It's the Romans who are to blame for this. No one else."

"Years ago, the tribes agreed to not rebel against the Romans for peace. And we were living in peace until their rebellion."

"Prasutagus, they—"

"I'm chieftain of the tribe now," he interrupted, giving her a firm look. "I'll not have any more bloodshed. The Roman governor rides here tomorrow. He needs our pledge of loyalty, our word that we won't rebel again. If we don't, the Romans will attack our tribe—and possibly take us all as slaves."

Fury and fear roiled through her. She recalled the Roman soldiers who'd swarmed through the village, seizing all the weapons. How could their village take on hundreds of their soldiers? More?

She pressed her fingertips to her temple. Prasutagus was right. They'd have no choice but to pledge loyalty, though rage tightened her chest at the thought of kneeling before the very soldiers who'd murdered her father.

She felt the pressure of Prasutagus's gentle hands on her shoulders and looked up at him.

"I don't like it either, wife. But this is our only chance for peace."

He pressed a kiss to her forehead before leaving her alone to meet with the nobles.

Restless, Boudica left their home moments after him, making her way to the forest until she reached her favorite clearing, with the winding stream that snaked through it. She knelt down by the stream, gazing down at the dark waters. The spirit world met the earthly one in the waters; it was why her tribe left votive offerings to the gods in streams and rivers, in the hope that the gods would hear their prayers and grant them their desires. She saw several votive offerings winding their way down the stream; members of the tribe must have left them there before the battle.

But the gods had not answered their prayers. Not this time.

Hatred filled her as she thought of the Romans, the men who'd killed her father. She held onto the hatred, allowing it to chase away her grief. She reached into her hair, removing a bronze clip that bound her braids together. It served as her own votive offering that she tossed into the stream.

But instead of a prayer to the gods, she issued a silent promise.

One day I will avenge you, Father.

7

The Romans came to the village the next day, but this time, Boudica didn't cower behind Rozen—or her husband. This time, she stood proudly next to Prasutagus, dressed in her finest tunic, the golden torc around her neck matching the one Prasutagus wore, surrounded by the other nobles.

She watched with burning eyes as Governor Aulus Plautius and Catus Decianus rode into the central square, dismounting from their horses. Behind them, a military guard of at least one hundred soldiers stood on sharp alert.

Aulus and Catus approached her and Prasutagus. Boudica lowered her gaze to shield the hatred that must have shown in her eyes.

Prasutagus stepped forward, his smile polite, but his body stiff with tension.

"We pledge our renewed allegiance to Rome and Emperor Claudius. We renounce our rebellion and remain your ally. Nor will we ever rise up in arms against Rome," he said, his voice loud enough for every Roman soldier and hovering villager to hear.

A searing anger raged in Boudica's chest; she had to clench her fists at her sides to quell it. Aulus and Catus looked pleased as Prasutagus sank to his knees before them, and the other nobles followed suit.

For a defiant moment, Boudica considered remaining upright, to reach for the dagger she had hidden beneath her tunic and hurl it right at the Roman governor's heart, to watch with pleasure as he bled out.

But Prasutagus looked at her, and the silent plea in his eyes compelled her to move. She forced herself to her knees, lowering her head, her heart thundering in her chest.

"We accept your allegiance, King Prasutagus," Governor Plautius replied, his voice filled with imperiousness. There was a hesitant pause, before he continued, "And Queen Boudica."

"We have a feast prepared to celebrate our renewed allegiance," Prasutagus said, standing to approach the Romans, his hand outstretched in welcome.

Boudica climbed to her feet, but remained where she was, keeping her gaze trained on the ground. Prasutagus had told her she wasn't required to dine with the Romans, they'd only requested the male nobles at the feast. In the past, that would have angered Boudica, but now she was grateful. She couldn't have kept up the façade of politeness for much longer, not when she ached to sink her blade into the hearts of each Roman soldier.

Boudica would soon come to learn that this was a desire that didn't abate even after the Romans left the village—a desire that would never abate.

AS THE DAYS WORE ON, GROWING COLDER WITH the passing of the season, Boudica watched Prasutagus become accustomed to his new role as chieftain. He wasn't as formidable as her father had been, but the tribe listened to him and respected him; Mael told her he made wise decisions for someone so young. He listened to conflicts between farmers and resolved them amicably; he bequeathed property of fallen warriors to deserving men of the tribe; he even patiently listened to the villagers' increasing grievances with the Romans, though as their pledged ally, there wasn't much he could do about those particular complaints.

While Prasutagus tended to his duties as chieftain, Boudica's days fell into a comfortable routine. She rose at first light and helped the attendants with the morning meal, which she would share with Prasutagus. She would then spend the majority of her day practice fighting with the strongest warriors of the tribe. Prasutagus not only allowed her to fight, he encouraged her to resume her practicing. When she'd completed her fighting for the day, she would attend the meetings Prasutagus held with the nobles and villagers, pride swelling in her chest as she watched how well he handled tribal matters. He would welcome her council about certain matters when they were alone, often taking her advice.

After he'd handle his duties as chieftain for the day, they would take long walks through the forest at night before supper, discussing the details of their day. He kept to his word and never pressured her to lie with him, only holding her in his arms at night. Boudica eagerly awaited their time alone together; their dinners, their walks through the forest, even his holding her at night. It became more difficult to deny the desire she felt for him, the burgeoning love she suspected had always been there.

On the night of Samhain, after she and Prasutagus spent the day presiding over ritual feasts and celebrations, Boudica slipped off her tunic before they went to bed, standing before him in the firelight of the hearth.

Prasutagus stilled, his amber eyes drifting down her nude body. Desire filled his gaze as he took a step toward her.

"Are you certain?" he whispered.

"Yes," Boudica replied, her heart hammering as

she moved closer to him, shyly disrobing him of his cloak and tunic. She could no longer quell her desire for her handsome husband, nor did she want to.

Prasutagus seized her mouth with his, and the warmth that often flowed through her at his touch flared into a fiery heat. He was gentle with her as he placed her down onto their bed of animal furs, and the brief sharp pain she felt when his body joined with hers soon melded away into pleasure.

After that first night, her physical hunger for Prasutagus grew, along with the love that had come to life inside her like a powerful flame, consuming every part of her.

"I will love you, only you," he whispered one night, after a breathless joining, capturing her face with his hands. "I will never take another wife."

Boudica's heart soared. She smiled, pressing her lips to his.

"I love you," she returned. "And if you had taken another wife, I'd have speared her with my blade."

He chuckled softly before claiming her lips with his.

I<small>T WAS THE EVE OF ANOTHER</small> B<small>ELTAINE WHEN</small> her monthly bleeding didn't come. When another month passed, and still she did not bleed, she went to see Rozen, who pressed her hands to her belly before calling for two druid healers.

"Praise Damara," one of the healers whispered, after she examined Boudica. "A babe grows in your belly."

Boudica stiffened and placed a hand to her belly. She'd never desired a child, but now a sudden and overwhelming love swelled within her. She left Rozen's home, hurrying through the village to find Prasutagus.

He was in their home with several nobles, but he dismissed them when he saw the look on her face.

"What is it?" he asked with a concerned frown.

She smiled, joy flowing through her, joy she hadn't thought she would ever feel again after her father's death.

"I'm with child."

Prasutagus's worried expression transformed to one of awe, of love. His eyes filled with tears, and he sank to his knees before her, lifting her tunic to kiss the bare flesh of her stomach.

"Our child," he whispered. "Our son." He looked up at her, his amber eyes shimmering. "I love you, wife."

"I love you, husband."

Mael and several druid priests came to their home that night to praise the goddess Damara and bless their unborn child, and Boudica made a quiet promise to herself. She resolved to put aside her desire for revenge against the Romans, along with her desire to become a warrior. She told herself that her unborn son was her duty to the tribe, and the best way to honor her father.

Yet a trace of defiance lingered, a defiance she couldn't quell. It remained deep within her heart, like kindling wood, waiting to be ignited.

II

60 CE

The Chieftain's Wife

8

Camulodunum, Britannia
Governor's Residence

Suetonius stood opposite Emperor Nero's personal advisor Lucius, attempting to keep his expression neutral as Lucius unfurled a sheet of papyrus, one that contained a personal message from Nero himself. The cool breeze drifted in from the open doorways of the triclinium, prickling at his skin. Britannia was cooler than he was used to, even in the warmer months, unlike the town of his youth, Pisaurum, on the coast of the Adriatic Sea, or the locale of his last governorship, the warm mountainous region of Mauretania. But he resisted the urge to tug his cloak close around him; he didn't want to show even the slightest weakness in front of the emperor's advisor.

Lucius had traveled all the way from Rome to

Camulodunum, the Roman capital in Britannia, to deliver a personal message from the emperor. Suetonius suspected the message was not a good one.

As Lucius studied the letter he'd unfurled, Suetonius realized that he looked eerily similar to the emperor: slight framed, blond hair, clear blue eyes. He wondered if Lucius was one of Nero's many rumored lovers. It wouldn't surprise him if Nero had taken a lover who looked like himself, given his self-aggrandization.

"Governor Suetonius Paulinus," Lucius said, reading Nero's words. "My great-uncle Emperor Claudius held you in great regard. He once told me the barbarian tribes you govern treat you with respect, more so than the previous governor. Yet the barbarian priests, the druids, still incite the northern tribes to rise against Rome. The barbarians greatly respect these druids; I feel you have not done enough to stop them."

Suetonius's mouth tightened; it took great effort to not show his contempt for Nero's words. Nero knew nothing of what it took to govern a province; he'd been coddled since the day he was born. Yet because he was a great-great-grandson of the god Emperor Augustus, he liked to think he had innate rulership skills. *He's grown more arrogant—and less rational—since having his own mother killed,* Suetonius thought, with a rush of anger. Suetonius was in his fortieth year and he'd governed two provinces. He knew far more of ruling than Nero.

But he gave Lucius a nod to continue, hoping that he looked properly chastised.

Lucius turned his focus to Catus Decianus, who stood at Suetonius's side. Anxiety over Nero's message had so consumed Suetonius that he'd forgotten the other man stood at his side.

"Catus Decianus. Claudius made you procurator of Britannia to manage its wealth, yet it barely brings enough coin or grain to feed our soldiers," Lucius read. "Rome's coffers decrease, while you grow wealthy from the tributes of the native tribes."

Catus stiffened, his ruddy face going pale. Suetonius had to hide a smile, pleased that Catus's greed had not gone unnoticed. Suetonius disliked Catus for this greed, and for his casual and unnecessary cruelty to the natives of Britannia.

Catus wasn't loyal to Rome—nor to anyone—but himself. He didn't know how a man like Catus had climbed up the ranks to become procurator; Suetonius suspected he'd done so in unscrupulous ways.

"You are ordered to bring in more coin from the province, or I shall replace you. As for you, Governor, I must remind you how important Britannia was to my great-uncle. It is therefore of great importance to me, and I will not be satisfied until it is entirely subdued. You will go to the druid sanctuary on the western isle of Mona, and you will slaughter them all."

All mirth faded from Suetonius. He'd just returned from two campaigns against rebellious tribes in the west. He considered protesting, to tell Lucius that slaughtering the druid priests would only inflame the barbarians and give them another reason to rally against Rome.

But this would be foolish. It was his advisors who had Nero's ear in Rome; nothing Suetonius could say from a distant province would sway the emperor's mind. Young upstarts such as Lucius would concede to any of Nero's demands. He wished that he could talk to Nero in person, but the journey from Britannia to Rome would take too much time.

"I demand to hear from you both after you carry out my orders," Lucius concluded.

He lowered the letter, eyeing Suetonius for a long moment, as if daring him to protest, before his gaze slid to Catus. Catus looked pleased by the order, giving Lucius a wide smile. Suetonius knew that Catus would happily carry out the order himself. He hated the natives and especially their priests, whom he called "mindless savages who think they know the wills of the gods."

But Suetonius, who'd never questioned an order, carrying it out with the same ease as he took his next breath, was filled with tumult. His duties as governor of Britannia had begun to place a strain on him, and a lingering malaise had seeped into his bones, a malaise he could not shake.

"Thank you, Lucius," he said, forcing a smile. "Inform the emperor that I will do as he commands. I will organize a contingent of men and we'll make our way north. You must be tired from your journey," he continued, gesturing to a hovering slave in the corner to come forward. "There are guest quarters prepared for you."

Once the slave led Lucius out of the triclinium, Catus's polite smile vanished, and he glowered.

"Presumptuous son of a whore," he sneered. "I fill Rome's coffers with taxes from the barbarians. Nero should be grateful."

Suetonius said nothing. He didn't want to share confidence with Catus; they were certainly not friends. His own thoughts were still turbulent, reeling from the harshness of Nero's order to slaughter the druid priests.

"You will heed his order," Suetonius muttered, rubbing his temples. "Visit with the friendly tribes, including the Trinovantes and the Iceni. The client king, Prasutagus, is amenable."

"I will not negotiate with the barbarians," Catus said with a scowl.

"Those tribes are our allies," Suetonius returned. "And they shall remain so. They understand they are clients of Rome, but be diplomatic in how you discuss taxing more of their grain."

He didn't need Catus to stir up conflict with the southern tribes, not while he was away in Mona. He'd feasted with their king, Prasutagus, and his nobles when he'd first become governor. Prasutagus was agreeable, but he recalled how his wife, Queen Boudica, had glared at him, her hatred barely concealed in her fiery green eyes. It was a look he'd seen in the eyes of many client queens and kings, anger they tried to hide; they knew the price for not being agreeable allies to Rome.

Catus's mouth tightened, but he nodded his agreement.

"You have guest quarters as well, if you wish to remain for the night after you dine," he said, though he prayed Catus would leave.

"I thank you," Catus said, his voice strained. Suetonius suspected he also wanted to leave, but it would be in poor form to not dine with Nero's personal advisor.

A second slave escorted Catus out, and Suetonius moved to the corner of the triclinium. He poured himself a cup of wine before a hovering slave had the chance to do it for him. Suetonius was not like Emperor Nero, or even Catus, who spent much of their time in luxurious residences, their every need tended to by slaves. At his core he was a soldier, and before Nero had appointed him as governor, that was where he was most comfortable—on a battlefield, following and doling out orders without hesitation.

He took another swig of wine, hoping that it would drown out the memories from his last campaign, when he and his soldiers subdued several rebelling tribes. In his dreams, he could still hear the screams of the barbarians and their pleas for mercy.

Suetonius closed his eyes. He'd not been able to sleep properly since that campaign, and now he had to leave for another, to slay a group of unarmed priests.

But he reminded himself of the oath he'd pledged as a young soldier, the *sacramentum militare*.

"The soldiers swear that they shall faithfully execute all that the emperor commands, that they shall never desert the service, and they shall not seek to avoid death for the Roman republic."

He would do his duty.

9

Boudica stood in the doorway of the chieftain's home, a smile tugging at her lips as she watched her two daughters practice fight with sticks.

Her eldest daughter, Brighid, in her twelfth year, circled around her sister, holding her large stick like a sword. Boudica had named her after a fire goddess and the name was fitting. Brighid reminded Boudica of herself at that age, in both looks and temperament; she had the same flame-red hair and eyes the color of jade; she was spirited and told her mother she had dreams of becoming a warrior.

Her younger daughter Nolwenn, in her tenth year, was the image of Prasutagus, with his dark hair and amber eyes; she also possessed his innate kindness. While Brighid longed to be a warrior, Nolwenn had a fondness for storytelling and wanted to become a bard.

Love swelled within Boudica's chest as she watched her daughters giggle, clashing their sticks together like swords. It was the same love that coursed through her when she first felt them kick in her womb, when she grew swollen with them, and when she birthed them, red-faced and screaming, as if protesting their births to the gods.

Twelve summers had passed since Boudica was a defiant girl of seventeen. Over the years, she allowed the love she felt for her daughters and for Prasutagus to cool her burning hatred for the Romans to a low simmer, and she barely noticed that it still lingered.

Prasutagus approached, coming to stand at Boudica's side, a smile curving his lips as he watched the girls. He'd grown from boy to man over the years; specks of gray peppered his dark hair and long mustache, and faint lines creased the skin around his eyes and mouth. But to Boudica he was still that young man in his nineteenth year whom she would sneak off to practice fight with, whom she now loved with the same ferocity she loved her girls.

He pulled her into the circle of his arms, and she leaned in close to him as they watched their daughters in companionable silence. Mael and the druid healers had predicted she would birth strong sons; she'd feared two daughters would disappoint Prasutagus. But when he first held Brighid and Nolwenn in his arms, his eyes had filled with tears and he gazed at them with nothing but love in his eyes.

Prasutagus released Boudica to approach the girls with an encouraging smile.

"Slow down," he urged, as Brighid's stick broke upon impact with Nolwenn's. He reached down to pick up another stick, handing it to Brighid.

"But yesterday you told me to move faster when I fought," Brighid protested.

"Only when you're defending yourself," Prasutagus said gently. He knelt to adjust their positions.

"I was winning," Brighid said with a frown

"No, you weren't," Nolwenn returned.

"Winning doesn't always matter, girls. It's about how well you fight," Prasutagus said.

Boudica smiled at their exchange, but the sound of weeping from the village square tore her attention away. She turned, freezing as she noticed several Roman soldiers round up a group of male villagers. The soldiers had come to their village earlier that day to conscript more men into the vast Roman army, but Boudica hadn't noticed their presence until now.

She'd seen such scenes many times over the years. The Romans would march into their village and round up the healthy men of the tribe to join their legions. The first time they'd come, she had to force herself to stand still and silent as the men were taken away, though she'd wanted to scream in protest.

We have no choice, Prasutagus had told her that first time. *If our men don't go with them by choice, they'll round them up by force. We are a client tribe, beholden to their empire.*

Anger held Boudica rigid as she watched a group of wives and mothers weep as the Romans led their husbands and sons out of the square. Kensa hurried into the square to comfort a weeping young wife.

Boudica's heart clenched as she studied Kensa. Kensa's husband, Arthek, had died in a Roman campaign four summers ago. Her grief was so great that she'd refused to ever take another husband. She'd taken up fostering other noble children, including Boudica's, as Rozen had done for them. The liveliness Kensa possessed in her youth had faded, and only a shadow of the girl she'd once been remained.

Kensa met Boudica's eyes across the square; she gave her a brief nod of acknowledgment before returning her attention to the crying woman in her arms, stroking her hair.

Prasutagus joined her side as the girls again began to fight with their sticks. He followed her gaze and tensed.

Boudica knew she should hold her tongue; she and Prasutagus had gotten into many arguments concerning the Romans over the years. It was the only major source of disagreement between them. As the chieftain's wife, it wasn't her place to advise him on how to handle the Romans; she'd seen the disapproval in the eyes of the nobles when she voiced any opinion about them. But it was difficult to keep quiet about the continual injustices their tribe suffered at the hands of the Romans.

"The Romans continue to conscript our men to

fight in their campaigns, even though we have already lost many," Boudica whispered. "Soon we will be a tribe of women and old men."

"It is what we agreed to in the alliance," Prasutagus said, his mouth tight. "I will discuss this no further, wife."

Defiance surged through Boudica, but she forced it to subside. Prasutagus was not like other husbands; he listened to her and took her council when it came to matters of the tribe. Yet with the Romans he was unbendable; it was the only time he reminded her of her status beneath him as his wife.

Prasutagus was called away by a fellow noble. He gave her a firm look before leaving, and Boudica set aside her lingering anger, telling the girls it was time for them to head to Kensa's home.

Boudica hadn't wanted to send the girls to live with a foster mother, even if it was Kensa, but Prasutagus insisted. Fostering was simply the way of the tribe, a way for sons and daughters to prepare for adult life outside of their own parents' home. The chief's daughters were no exception to the tradition. Though Boudica saw her daughters every day and came over to Kensa's home to share meals with them, it was still difficult for her to part with them.

As Boudica walked with her girls across the village square to Kensa's home, she took it in. The village had grown larger since she was a girl, and though roundhouses and farmsteads still filled it, the Roman presence was evident in the paved roads that crisscrossed the village along with several stone and brick buildings. She felt the Roman buildings were stains on what had been a purely Icenian village, but kept silent about her dislike to Prasutagus.

Kensa was waiting for them in the doorway of her home. Prasutagus had offered her the home of a deceased noble after her husband died, but Kensa had refused, wanting to remain in the home she'd shared with Arthek.

Kensa's smile was wide as the girls approached. Boudica only saw Kensa with such a joyful smile when she was around her daughters; she loved them as if they were her own. Kensa embraced Brighid and Nolwenn before ushering them both inside.

"The Romans took Breok's son," Kensa said in a low voice to Boudica, once the girls had disappeared inside. "Breok lost her last two sons in Roman campaigns. She pleaded with them to spare her only son. The soldiers nearly struck her to silence her cries."

Anger flared once more inside Boudica, as Kensa continued, "The villagers are angry. Many are planning to meet with Prasutagus and the nobles to air their grievances about the Romans tomorrow. It's not just about them recruiting us into their armies. It's the grain shortages as well."

Boudica expelled a sigh. The Romans taxed the tribe's grain, even though there had been shortages as of late.

"I've tried talking to my husband about the Romans," Boudica said, with a prickling of guilt.

"No one blames you nor the chieftain for what the Romans do," Kensa said swiftly, reaching out to grasp Boudica's hand. Her expression darkened. "We know what happens if the chieftain doesn't obey their commands."

A chilled silence fell between them. Tribes who didn't obey the Romans were subdued: taken into slavery or killed.

"Enough talk of the Romans," Kensa said, waving her hand in the air and smiling, though it was forced. "Stay for awhile. We can have mead by the hearth. We won't disturb your daughters' sleep—they could sleep through dozens of rowdy combat challenges."

After the girls were settled into their beds of furs and had drifted off to sleep, Boudica and Kensa sat by the hearth with a shared cup of mead. When it was just her and Kensa, Boudica felt as if she was still a young woman living under Rozen's roof, with no husband and children.

A pang pierced her at the thought of her foster mother. Rozen had joined the gods the same year Kensa's husband died. She'd suffered from no visible illness; Mael had told her it was simply old age and time for her to pass on to the next life. Rozen had been at Boudica's side for the births of her two daughters and had kept watch over them when she, Kensa, or her attendants could not. Boudica still missed her foster mother's guidance.

"Do you think he's waiting for me?" Kensa whispered, pulling Boudica from the maelstrom of her thoughts.

Boudica turned to face her friend. Kensa's eyes shone with tears as she gazed at the crackling fire of the hearth. "My Arthek. Do you think he's waiting for me with the gods?"

"Yes," Boudica said, taking Kensa's hand.

In the past, Boudica had tried to comfort Kensa over Arthek's death with words, but she now understood that Kensa just wanted her ear, that words could never fill the void of grief. And so they sat in silence, with only the crackling sounds of the fire and her daughters' soft breathing to fill it.

"There's a man who wishes to wed me," Kensa said finally. "Elouan. He's a craftsman. His wife joined the gods two winters ago. He made me this," she added, fingering a fine bronze brooch pinned to her tunic. "Elouan is handsome and so very kind. Whenever I see him, I feel a warmth I haven't felt since Arthek was alive. And . . . I feel guilty for it."

"Arthek wouldn't want you to spend the rest of your days alone," Boudica said. "You have many years ahead of you."

"That's what I keep telling myself. I told him I need time. I never thought I'd wed again."

Guilt swirled through Boudica's chest. She should have insisted that Prasutagus stand up to the Romans about conscription into their armies. If

Arthek hadn't been conscripted, he'd still be alive and by Kensa's side. She squeezed Kensa's hand.

"You should allow yourself happiness."

A sudden rush of determination filled her. Tomorrow, she would attend the villagers' meeting with Prasutagus. Something had to change about their forced alliance with the Romans. If it became necessary, Boudica would be the one to force that change.

Boudica slipped into the meeting hall the next morning, careful to remain in the back. Prasutagus wouldn't want her here. After their last argument about the Romans, he'd forbidden her from attending tribal meetings regarding them.

Now, Prasutagus stood in front of the gathered villagers as they addressed him all at once. Though his expression was calm, his body was rigid with tension.

Mael stood at his side. Now in his fifties, with gray dusting his dark hair and fine wrinkles around his eyes, he was still the same mysterious priest who'd intimidated Boudica when she was younger. He served as Prasutagus's advisor as he'd advised her father; Prasutagus told her that his input was invaluable, and beneath the mask of stoicism that Mael wore, he was a thoughtful and compassionate man.

"Many of our crops have failed for the season,

Chieftain Prasutagus," Ronat was saying. Ronat was a farmer she'd known since she was a girl; he used to give her sugar beets that grew on his lands as a treat during Beltaine celebrations. He was now an old man, standing hunched, supported by his eldest son. "We barely have enough to eat for ourselves. And they want us to give them our crops as tax?"

"We're beholden to the Romans—" Prasutagus began.

Loud shouts of protest from the villagers interrupted him, and Boudica stiffened. She'd never seen such a negative reaction to Prasutagus's words at a tribal meeting.

"If you can't feed yourselves nor your families," Prasutagus said, raising his voice over the shouts of protest, "then the nobles of the tribe have agreed to distribute food from the surplus."

"And what of the conscriptions?" asked Breok, the woman Kensa had comforted the day before. "They have taken all of my sons from me. I'm a widow—I have no one."

"My son has just come of age," said another villager, his face tight with fear. "Will they take him as well?"

"It is what we agreed to in the truce," Prasutagus said tersely. "I'm sorry—the conscriptions will continue."

"You have two daughters you will never lose in battle!" the villager spat. "That's why you're not concerned with the conscriptions!"

The villagers shouted their agreement. Boudica watched with growing unease.

Prasutagus stilled, his face tightening with anger. For a man who rarely displayed anger, it was an intimidating sight, and the villagers fell silent.

"Every man in this village is like a brother to me, or a father, or a son. I don't like the conscriptions." He met the eyes of each villager before continuing, "I'll talk to the Roman leader, Catus Decianus, when he next feasts here. I'll tell him how many men we've lost, and that our crops are failing. I can't promise that anything will change. But I'll share your concerns."

A sliver of hope filled Boudica, a hope that the other villagers seemed to share as the anger on their faces vanished. Prasutagus met her gaze across the hall, and she stiffened, but he didn't look angered by her presence. Instead, he gave her a wide smile, one which she returned.

She prayed the Romans would agree to their requests; they'd not resisted any of their demands after the failed uprising years before, and Catus seemed amiable toward Prasutagus, who treated him with diplomatic respect whenever he came to the village.

Boudica clung to this hope, like a warrior fighting for his last breath after being struck down in battle. Perhaps true peace, even under the rule of the Romans, was possible.

10

When the Romans came to feast, it took at least a dozen attendants to set up the chieftain's home for the soldiers; they cleaned the animal pelts, scrubbed the low wooden tables with lime until they gleamed. The tribal cooks used the best meats—meats usually reserved for ritual feasts—cooking them over slow-burning hearth fires, until the meat was succulent. Since the Romans preferred wine as drink; they used their best stores of wine, poured into individual cups as the Romans were accustomed to, rather than the communal cups used at their own feasts.

Yet even with all the preparations, Boudica often noticed the dismissiveness in the eyes of the Roman soldiers and Catus Decianus; she'd once overheard him bemoan having to dine with the "barbarians" for diplomatic purposes.

Women weren't usually invited to the feasts with

the Romans, for which Boudica was grateful. During the feasts Prasutagus did ask her to attend, she would sit with a strained smile, trying to ignore the pulsating anger that thrummed within her.

But tonight, Boudica would put aside her acrimony and attend the feast. She wanted to make certain that her husband spoke to Catus about the concerns of the tribe. It would be difficult, but she would force herself to sit quietly with the female nobles, a demure smile on her face for the sake of their guests, and prayed to Garmangabis, the goddess of fortune, that Catus would acquiesce to their requests.

The attendants usually prepared for the Roman feasts on their own, but this time she directed them, pointing out where she and the female nobles would sit, where Prasutagus and the nobles would sit, where the Romans would sit. She wanted to be close to Catus and her husband; she couldn't sit by his side with the Romans present, but she wanted to sit within hearing distance.

She feared that Prasutagus would forbid her to attend the feast, but he didn't protest as her attendants helped her get dressed. She wore her finest tunic, a blue one made of silk, along with the golden torc she wore for festivals. She wore her hair in one braid, pinned to her nape with a golden pin. She wanted to look royal tonight, to display her exalted place in the tribe.

As evening fell, Boudica stood at her husband's

side outside their home to greet Catus and his soldiers, who entered the village square on horseback. They dismounted as tribal attendants stepped forward to take their horses.

Boudica forced herself to smile, hating the way Catus's eyes roamed over her body with both lasciviousness and distaste. She made herself bow, along with Prasutagus. It irritated her that they had to bow, when they were royal, and Catus a mere Roman official. But she thought of the widows, of the mothers who lost their sons, of the starving families in their village, and she made certain to bow low. Now was not the time for pride. If she and Prasutagus were agreeable, perhaps he would show mercy.

"Is your queen joining us for the feast tonight?" Catus asked, his eyes still on her as he addressed Prasutagus.

"Yes. My wife and other nobles of the tribe wish to join us for our feast," Prasutagus replied with a smile.

"Very well," Catus said, continuing to gaze at her. "My men need something pretty to rest their eyes upon."

Disgust coiled through Boudica, but she kept her smile pinned on her face.

"We are pleased to dine with you," she said, in her stilted Latin.

Out of necessity, Prasutagus had learned the Roman tongue, and he'd insisted she learned some of their language as well for diplomatic purposes. But she rarely spoke Latin, preferring the softer and familiar lilt of the tribe's Brittonic tongue to Latin's hard-edged formality.

Catus's mouth twitched at her stilted use of his tongue, but he acknowledged her words with a nod. Prasutagus stepped forward, and the two men entered the home, followed by Boudica, her attendants, and Catus's soldiers.

During the meal, Boudica kept her eyes trained on Prasutagus and Catus, barely paying attention to the female nobles at her sides who tried to make conversation. Prasutagus and Catus's heads were bowed low together, as though they were old friends, smiling and nodding as they spoke in low tones. Catus even presented Prasutagus with a jug of sealed wine; he took it with a broad grin of gratitude.

Boudica's grip on her cup of wine tightened. She told herself that Prasutagus was merely doing his duty as chieftain; he had to be friendly with Catus. Her gaze slid to the Roman soldiers, and she noticed with unease that they were eyeing some of the women. She was relieved Kensa had opted not to attend the feast.

"The hour grows late. You should return to your homes," Boudica said, turning to the female nobles who sat around her, hoping that her tone sounded light.

The women heeded her order—Boudica suspected they'd also noticed the attention of the Roman soldiers—and dutifully filed out. Though several of the Roman soldiers shouted drunken protests, none of them demanded that the women stay, and relief filled her chest.

Boudica returned her focus to Catus and Prasutagus. She still couldn't hear whatever they were discussing, but the topic seemed to not be serious; they were both chuckling as Prasutagus took a large swig of the wine Catus had gifted him.

She let out a sharp breath, anger roiling through her. She didn't know when they'd next receive a visit from Catus. She had to do something.

Boudica forced herself to her feet. Squaring her shoulders, she folded her hands before her to hide their shaking. She stepped forward, approaching Prasutagus and Catus.

Everyone in the home fell silent; Boudica was keenly aware of every eye on her. Her pulse fluttered wildly at the base of her throat, but she was determined to see this through.

Prasutagus's entire body went tense as she approached.

"Wife—" he began.

"There's—there's something we need to ask of you," she interrupted, focusing her attention on Catus, hating how weak her voice sounded.

Catus put down his glass of wine, his lips curving in amusement as his gaze slid to Prasutagus.

"In Rome, I've seen wives flogged for intervening in the conversations of their husbands."

Catus's soldiers laughed. Fury whipped through

her, and she pulled herself to her full height, glowering down at him.

"This is not Rome."

Their laughter abruptly died, and tension crawled the walls of silence that filled the home. Catus's smile vanished, his round face tightening with fury.

"Boudica—" Prasutagus hissed, getting to his feet.

"Your grain taxes are a burden to our people," Boudica continued, still focused on Catus, whose face reddened with increased fury. "And the conscription of our men into your armies must end. We need our men here, to help toil our fields."

"I apologize for my wife, Catus," Prasutagus said. He turned to look at her, and she nearly recoiled from the fury in his eyes. "Wife. Leave here and go to Kensa's. At once."

Boudica looked at him in angry disbelief, but Prasutagus's expression was like granite. She didn't want to back down, but she could see that several of the Roman soldiers had shifted, as if they were about to rise.

She clenched her fists at her sides, wishing she had her sword. She imagined sinking it into Catus's heart and then all of his soldiers.

But she forced herself to turn and leave, Prasutagus's dismissal cutting through her like the sharp blade of a dagger.

The Romans remained until dawn. Boudica lay awake in Kensa's home, curled up in bed next to her daughters. Kensa and her daughters remained asleep, even though the drunken laughter and shouts of the Romans drifted all the way across the square into the home for most of the night.

Anger still coursed through her at Prasutagus's dismissal, anger which kept her awake throughout the night. She'd only spoken up for the sake of their tribe. Why couldn't Prasutagus do the same? How could he be so friendly with the usurpers of their lands?

Boudica waited until the sounds of the feast faded, and the hooves of the Roman horses pounded away from the village.

She slipped out of Kensa's home, tucking her cloak around her against the chill of the morning air.

She entered her and Prasutagus's home to find several attendants clearing away the low tables and food. Prasutagus stood by the hearth, staring into the dying flames. Prasutagus dismissed the attendants without turning around as soon as Boudica stepped inside.

"I spoke up for our tribe," Boudica said, once they were alone. Her anger rose as she approached him. "You were laughing with Catus as if he were your—"

"I know Catus. You don't. I had to make sure he was drunk and merry before I made any demands of him," Prasutagus snapped. "You should have trusted me. I've been chieftain for some time; I know what's best for the tribe."

Boudica tensed, a stab of guilt pricking her. He closed his eyes, finally turning to face her, his expression softening.

"I know you were only trying to help," he said. "Do you remember the time when we were children? I was in my twelfth year, you your ninth? We were running through the groves with some other children, and we all heard a noise coming from a yew bush."

Boudica frowned. She remembered the incident well, but didn't know what it had to do with last night's confrontation with Catus.

"Yes," she said. "But I don't—"

"Everyone—me, Kensa, and the other boys were all too scared to approach it," Prasutagus continued, moving toward her with a nostalgic smile. "But you went right toward the noise."

"I was shaking like a leaf," Boudica murmured, drawn in by the memory. "A hare leapt out at me. I went home crying to Rozen like a baby."

"But you were the only one brave enough to see what the sound was. That's how you looked tonight when you came over to us. Brave," Prasutagus said, a wary pride shining in his eyes. "I was angry at you—but proud. I could tell you were scared, but you spoke up anyway."

He reached for her hand and pulled her close.

"Catus will speak to the new governor, Suetonius Paulinus, about our tribe's concerns."

"He will?" Boudica breathed. "About the

conscriptions in the army? And the taxes on our grain?"

"He made no promises as to the outcome, but he said he'd send word about our shortages and lack of men. It could be some time before we see anything change—if anything changes at all. But at least—"

Boudica interrupted him, throwing her arms around him and pressing her lips to his.

"Thank you," she whispered, when she pulled back. "I'm sorry; I should have trusted you."

"I know I was harsh when I asked you to leave. But Catus was furious—I had to calm him by sending you away. Roman women . . . they're not treated as women are here. He's likely never had a woman confront him. And," Prasutagus continued, his voice dropping to a whisper, "I think he's frightened of you."

They both chuckled before Prasutagus leaned in to seize her lips with his.

"My fiery love. My wife," he whispered, before swinging her up into his arms.

They spent the rest of the morning making love, and when they fell asleep in each other's arms, spent from their lovemaking and their sleepless night, the hope in Boudica's heart was once again reignited.

Later, Boudica would recall every detail of the rest of that day. The midday meal she and

Prasutagus shared with their daughters. The succulent pork meat that stuck to her fingers from the honey it had been roasted in. Nolwenn repeating tales she'd learned from the bards. Brighid showing them fight moves a warrior had taught her. The walk she took with Nolwenn and Brighid into the surrounding woodlands—when Prasutagus was called away to take care of tribal matters—showing them the clearing where she and Prasutagus once held their practice fights. Kensa introducing her and her daughters to Elouan, the man who wanted to wed her, a handsome dark-haired man with kind eyes, when she dropped the girls off at Kensa's home for the night. And finally, the kiss she and Prasutagus shared before they both drifted off to sleep, and the warmth of his arms as he pulled her close.

That night, strange images filled Boudica's dreams. In one dream, she stood in the center of a vast field surrounded on all sides by woodlands. As she looked around, disconcerted, she realized the field was edged with blazing fires and soaked with blood. She took in her trembling hands: blood covered them. When she looked back up, the field was no longer empty.

She stumbled back, horror coursing through her. Dead bodies now littered all parts of the field.

Boudica awoke with a strangled cry, unnerved by the vivid nightmare. She took several breaths, taking in her surroundings to calm herself. The crackling fire of the hearth. The crickets chirping outside. Prasutagus sleeping at her side.

Calmed, she lay back down to curl into the warmth of her husband's arms. But she stilled, studying Prasutagus closely.

His breathing was pained and ragged, his skin eerily pale. Boudica sat up, gently nudging him awake.

"Prasutagus..."

Prasutagus opened his eyes, those amber eyes she loved, but they were wild and unfocused. He opened his mouth to speak, but no words came.

He coughed up blood.

11

Fear seized Boudica as she watched Mael and a healer tend to her husband. Dawn had broken, and faint sunlight from the opening in the thatch roof spilled into their home, casting Prasutagus in a faint light. His eyes were shut, his breathing quick and shallow. Mael pressed his hands to the sides of Prasutagus's flushed face, then to his chest. He spoke quiet words to the healer before standing to approach Boudica.

Kensa stood at her side, gripping her hand. She'd come soon after Mael and the healer had arrived and remained fixedly at Boudica's side. Boudica was grateful for her friend's presence, and she tightened her hold on Kensa's hand as Mael drew near.

"His fever grows worse," Mael said, his voice grim. "We fear he won't survive the day."

Shock spiraled through Boudica; she feared her

knees would give way. Only Kensa's steady hold kept her upright.

"No," Boudica whispered, shaking her head. Her husband was vibrant and in good health, fitter than most warriors of the tribe. He had many years ahead of him. He'd rarely fallen ill in all the years she'd known him and recovered quickly from any minor ailment that struck him.

"He—he showed no sign of illness before," she continued. "He was in good health. It wasn't until after the feast that he—"

She faltered, a terrible thought striking her. *The feast.*

"Did my husband drink or eat anything no one else had?" she asked, probing through the haze of her shock to her memories of the night before. She'd watched her husband and Catus closely; she would have noticed if Catus or someone else had slipped him poison.

"The Romans brought wine only for the chieftain . . . as a gift. It's custom. No one else had the wine," Mael said, his skin going ashen.

At her side, Kensa let out a soft cry, pressing her hand to her mouth. Boudica closed her eyes, fighting past her panic, searching for hope amid the frantic thoughts that raced through her mind.

"He needs to be checked for signs of poison," Boudica said, trying to keep her voice steady. "Perhaps there's an antidote we can—"

"If the chieftain was poisoned, it'll be difficult to

tell what poison was used," Mael gently interrupted. "But we will try. Of that you have my promise."

Mael ducked his head in a bow and turned to rejoin the healer. Boudica trailed him, kneeling by Prasutagus's side as they pressed a jug of water to his lips, moistened his flushed and heated skin with damp fabric, placed healing herbs into his mouth.

Boudica stayed at his side, even after Mael and the healer left Prasutagus alone to rest, though he remained feverish and unconscious.

Day stretched into night, and her muscles ached from being seated for so long, but still she didn't move from his side.

"Boudica."

Boudica looked up. Kensa approached, kneeling down next to her. She'd been so consumed with tending to Prasutagus that she hadn't noticed it was now the dead of night; beyond the open doorway of the home she only saw blackness; no sound came from the surrounding village.

"You've not eaten," Kensa said, her face creased with worry.

"I'll not leave him."

"You must take care of yourself too. Your girls . . . they hear rumors their father is ill. They're confused and scared. They need their mother. You can't make yourself ill with worry."

At the mention of her girls, Boudica stilled. Her daughters had been on her mind, entangled with worry for Prasutagus, but she determined that she wouldn't needlessly worry them. Prasutagus wouldn't die; the gods were not that cruel.

"Tell them that he's ill, but he will get better," she said, her tone firm.

"Boudica—"

"Leave us."

Kensa hesitated but set down a jug of water at Boudica's side before leaving her.

Boudica lifted the jug to her dry lips, savoring the rush of liquid into her parched throat. Keeping her hand in Prasutagus's cold one, she curled up next to him.

"You will not die," she whispered to his unconscious form as fatigue claimed her. "I won't allow it."

SHE AWOKE TO A GENTLE PRESSURE ON HER shoulder. Mael knelt by her side, lifting his hand from her shoulder when she sat up, blinking her lethargy away.

By the dim sunlight she could tell that it was just past first light. She turned to look down at Prasutagus; he was as still as he'd been the night before. The same healer from before tended to him, dabbing his face with wet fabric, pressing a jug to his parched lips.

Mael gestured for her to follow him. She stumbled to her feet, drawing her cloak around her as she trailed him to the far corner of the home.

"From the scent of his breath, the healer did detect faint traces of poison," Mael whispered.

Rage filled her chest, pulling her from her lingering fatigue. She closed her eyes against the sting of tears, clenching her hands into fists at her sides.

"Why?" she whispered. She knew the Romans were treacherous, but what they'd done defied logic. Prasutagus had been nothing but loyal to the Romans. "Why would they poison him?"

"Catus is filled with greed," Mael said, his expression darkening. "With the chieftain out of the way, he could have Rome raise taxes for the tribe—and fill his own coffers."

"He poisoned my husband for coins?" Boudica seethed, her anger spiking. "When my husband wakes, I'll tell him of this treachery."

"Boudica." Mael's voice was gentle but firm. "The poison is from the henbane plant. We know of no antidote to this poison. It will take him."

Boudica opened her mouth to protest, but no words came. Deep in her heart, she knew he spoke the truth. The Romans wouldn't have poisoned Prasutagus with something easy to cure.

"The gods must will his return, child," Mael continued. "When your husband has joined the gods, you will be the new leader of the tribe, along with Rome, until your daughters come of age. The chieftain has decreed it in his will. And then—"

"I won't rule my tribe with Rome," Boudica spat.

"And my husband still lives. Don't speak of him as if he's already joined the gods."

"But he soon will," Mael said, his tone rigid. "You must accept it. The tribe will look to you for leadership. I . . . am sorry, Boudica."

Boudica stood alone as Mael left her side, grief coiling around her, and she had to reach out to grab the wall to hold herself steady.

Memories flooded her mind like the fierce rush of a downhill stream: Prasutagus training her how to fight, Prasutagus's loving amber eyes trained on hers when Mael wed them all those years ago, Prasutagus's naked flesh pressed against hers as they made their daughters, his eyes filled with love, joy, desire, Prasutagus standing before the nobles as he was officially made chieftain, and Prasutagus holding their daughters in his arms, gazing at them with a reverence usually reserved only for the gods.

Boudica sank against the wall, allowing herself to weep, pressing her face into her hands.

When her tears subsided, she pushed herself away from the wall and called for an attendant. She made herself eat the bread and ale the attendant brought her, though the food tasted like wood. But she needed to eat. The past day had been for her grief as a wife. Mael was right; now it was time to put her grief aside. She was a mother and leader of the tribe.

Boudica asked the attendant to bring her daughters to her and changed into a fresh tunic and cloak. She made herself wear the heavy golden torc that the chieftain and his kin wore, to show her people they had a leader still, a strong one, even though she wanted nothing more than to curl up and allow her grief to consume her.

When her daughters arrived, she stepped outside to meet them, kneeling down to their height.

"Your father is very ill," she said, taking care to keep her voice gentle. "He—he will soon join the gods."

Nolwenn's eyes widened before she dissolved into tears, throwing herself into Boudica's arms. She pulled Nolwenn close, allowing her daughter to weep into the crook of her neck.

But while Nolwenn dissolved, Brighid remained solid, going still as a rock. Boudica probed her eyes; she could tell that she was trying to fight back her tears.

"He may not hear you . . . but now is the time to say your goodbyes," Boudica forced herself to say when Nolwenn's tears subsided. She stood, before grief splintered her into two, reminding herself that it would do no good to fall apart in front of the girls.

The healer left them alone as they entered. Brighid and Nolwenn stilled at the sight of their father; they were used to seeing him healthy and strong. Nolwenn pressed her hands to her mouth, weeping into her palms as she approached him. Brighid trailed her sister, her green eyes glistening with tears.

Nolwenn knelt at Prasutagus's side, taking his

hand. Prasutagus stirred, as if sensing his daughters were near. His eyes fluttered, and Boudica's heart leapt into her throat. She'd feared that in his delirium he wouldn't wake—and if he did, he wouldn't recognize them.

But he smiled, that smile she so loved, and gripped Nolwenn's hand before reaching out to take Brighid's. Tears burned Boudica's eyes as he whispered to them, words Boudica couldn't hear, before kissing their foreheads and holding them in his arms for a long moment before releasing them.

Her attendant led her daughters out, but before they left Boudica knelt before them, whispering that she would visit them later, wiping away their tears with her fingers and embracing them once more.

She moved to Prasutagus's side, taking his cold hand and pressing it to the side of her face. His eyes fluttered; he was fighting to keep them open. She reached down, pressing the jug of water to his lips. He drank in several large swallows, never taking his eyes off her. He opened his mouth to speak.

"Quiet, husband," she whispered, lowering the jug to the floor. "You need to rest."

"My mind's fading. I need you to listen..."

He gestured for her to lean in closer. As she did so, he wound his fingers in her hair, holding her gaze.

"Whatever caused this illness . . . I do not want vengeance. I want you to live a long and happy life with our girls."

Boudica froze, astonishment spiraling through

her. He'd already surmised that Catus had poisoned him and that she ached for revenge. He knew her too well. It was why she loved him with every fiber of her being.

"Wife." Prasutagus's voice was weak yet determined. "I need your word."

Boudica held his gaze, wishing he made her keep any other promise. Any other promise that she would be happy to keep. But how could she deny him anything in this moment, one of his last, before he joined the gods?

"You have my promise," she whispered.

Prasutagus's eyes shut, and the tension seemed to drain from his body.

"Keep careful watch over Brighid. She's just like you. Spirited, headstrong. And our Nolwenn . . . always telling tales. She'll make a fine bard."

Boudica pressed her hand to her mouth, tears spilling from her eyes.

"I will. Husband," she whispered, squeezing his hand, "we deserved a lifetime."

"Even that wouldn't have been enough, my love. Not for me."

Boudica smiled through her tears. He was right. Only an eternity would have been enough time with Prasutagus.

"I never should've denied my love for you when I was a foolish girl." She reached down to take his hand, pressing it to her lips. She held his gaze, needing him to carry her next words with him when he left this earthly world to join the gods. "As long as I breathe, I'll never love another."

She leaned down, pressing her forehead to his. His skin was damp and feverish, but she relished its feel. The feel of him. Her Prasutagus. Her love.

And she remained at his side for the rest of the day and night, laying entwined with him, until he drew his last, ragged breath.

12

Isle of Mona

Suetonius sat astride his horse, surveying the remote marshy island on the western shores of Britannia, covered only by sparse woodlands. This was the isle of Mona, a sacred place for the barbarian priests. It was here that they trained and carried out their rituals. It was also here that they harbored fugitives who'd fled from the Romans.

A contingent of several hundred soldiers surrounded him. They'd made the difficult journey north from their various posts throughout the lands in the south, dismounting when necessary to trudge their horses through the damp and swampy fields and ancient roads that were not yet paved. He could tell by the pallor of their skin and the shadows beneath their eyes that his soldiers were weary from the long journey, but they knew their mission here was a direct order from Nero.

Suetonius tightened his grip on the reins of his horse as the druid priests emerged from the trees, clad in white ritual robes, though some were nude, their bodies covered in tattoos. They bellowed out shouts and cries in their tongue, working themselves up into a frenzy, as he'd seen other barbarian armies do right before an attack. But unlike those tribal cries, these were prayers. He only knew snatches of the Brittonic tongue, but he recognized the names of several gods.

"So these are the fabled druids."

Suetonius glanced to his side. His general, Tertius, a young soldier who was all hard muscles and arrogance, and reminded him of himself when he was younger, smirked at the sight of the frenzied druids.

"These are the barbarian priests who incite the tribes to rebellion with their 'great wisdom'?" Tertius spat on the ground, shaking his head. "They believe they can divine the future from the entrails of the dead. Have they divined their own slaughter? And what is that nonsense they're shouting?"

Tertius turned to Suetonius with a grin, but Suetonius didn't return it. He turned back to study the druids, realizing their display of fervor was just for appearances sake. Their numbers were low; he estimated only one or two hundred. They were no match for the trained soldiers he had at his command.

And despite their aggressive show of frenzy, they were barely armed.

"They're prayers," Suetonius said quietly. "Prayers in their native tongue. Sacred communion with their gods."

Suetonius didn't realize how reverential he sounded until Tertius gave him a look of disbelief that bordered on disgust. Suetonius hardened his features, averting his gaze.

"Governor, we should not wait to attack," Tertius said finally. "Their numbers are small, but they know this island better than we do. Shall I give the order?"

Suetonius tensed. Tertius's words were a subtle challenge. Suetonius was the one who gave orders, not his second-in-command.

He shook himself from the odd hesitation that had seized him, riding his horse out to face his soldiers, leveling them with hard looks.

"These barbarian men and women are merely priests," he said, his voice loud enough to carry over the sound of the waves crashing against the shore and the bellowing druids behind them. "You are to make their deaths quick."

He expelled a breath and gave his men the order to charge.

13

Boudica looked down at Prasutagus's belongings, a hollow emptiness filling her. The attendants had placed them in the center of the home in chests: his torcs, tunics, cloaks, various brooches she'd given him as gifts over the years, crafts their daughters had made for him, and offerings from members of the tribe all filled the chest.

Ten nights had passed since Prasutagus's burial. During the ceremony, she'd stood stoically above his burial mound, clutching her daughters' hands as they wept while Mael sang songs of prayer before sending him off to the gods. She'd remained stoic as her daughters slept with her in the bed she'd once shared with Prasutagus, sobs shaking their young bodies. She'd remained stoic as she met with the nobles the day after his burial, as they gave her their agreement to Prasutagus's will, which called for his daughters to rule in his stead, and for Boudica to rule the tribe in his absence until they came of age.

Her stoicism had remained as the days wore on, days she filled with duties she had to tend to as interim ruler of the tribe. Her duties acted as a shield against the onslaught of grief that threatened to consume her. She saw the looks of pity on the faces of the villagers, but she didn't want their pity. She wanted her husband: her kind, handsome husband, whom she would love fiercely for the rest of her days.

She'd continued to maintain her mask of calm for her daughters, who wept for their father the first few nights after his burial.

"I'm going to share tales about Papa to the bards, so he will never be forgotten," Nolwenn whispered one night, when her tears subsided.

"We will never forget him," Boudica returned. "You, me, Brighid . . . all who loved him. That is what's most important."

Nolwenn had nodded, but Brighid said nothing, her red-rimmed eyes trained on the thatch roof above. She clutched a sheathed dagger in her hands, a dagger Prasutagus had gifted her during the last festival. While Nolwenn wept, Brighid displayed her grief through aggression; the day after Prasutagus's death she'd injured a warrior's son during a practice fight. The warrior and his son had been understanding and accepted Boudica's apology, seeming to understand that Brighid's grief was the cause, but

Boudica had forbidden her from sparring for the time being.

It was after her daughters slept that Boudica allowed her mask of calm to slip, and her grief and rage burned hot, emerging from the hollow shell of her heart. She wanted nothing more than to tear Catus's head from his body, to take pleasure in his screams of agony as she did so. But then she'd remember her promise to Prasutagus, to live in peace and not seek revenge, and she would force her rage to subside.

Kensa tried to comfort her, having lost her own husband. It was a dark kinship they shared now, having both lost their husbands to the Romans.

"I talk to my husband still—and not just at his burial mound," she'd told Boudica. "When I'm alone in our home, in the sacred groves, and by the streams where the villagers leave their votive offerings. It makes his loss less painful. I . . . I even told him about Elouan. I think you were right. He would have wanted me to be happy. As Prasutagus would want you to be happy."

But Boudica hadn't responded, wanting to scream that she didn't want to speak to empty air, that he shouldn't be gone, he should be alive and at her side, and that after losing him, she would never truly be happy again.

Now, taking in her husband's belongings before her, she swallowed. She'd stopped her attendants from touching them after his death, for once his possessions were gone, he was truly gone. She stilled as her gaze strayed to two daggers that rested next to the pile; she and Prasutagus had used these in practice fights during their youth.

She knelt down to pick one up, recalling one practice fight she'd had with Prasutagus when she was in her fourteenth year. He'd been training her how to fight with a dagger, but had outmaneuvered her every time, forcing her defeat. She'd thrown down her dagger in frustration.

"I don't want to fight with daggers. I'm better with the sword."

"Warriors are trained in all manner of weapons," Prasutagus had said. "You want to be a warrior one day, do you not?"

"Yes, but—"

"Let's try again."

She'd lost to him once more, and in her frustration she'd nearly stormed out of the clearing. But Prasutagus had grabbed her arm, preventing her from leaving. He'd then told her the same words he'd tell their daughters years later.

"Winning doesn't always matter. It's about how well you fight."

"Boudica."

Judoc's voice pulled her from memories of the past. She dashed away a stray tear and straightened, turning to find him standing by the doorway. Judoc had served as Prasutagus's main guard, now he was hers.

Though now in his fortieth year, he was still the same muscular and robust man who'd won many combat challenges in Boudica's youth. His eyes were shadowed; he'd had the same look since Prasutagus's death. He'd told her he blamed himself for the chieftain's death, for failing to protect him, despite her assurances there was nothing he could have done.

"The Romans are approaching the village," he said now, his expression tight with worry.

Boudica froze. Catus usually sent a messenger before he came for a feast or diplomatic visit. Rage filled her at the thought of Catus; if he was coming to the village, it would take all her strength to not run him through with her sword.

"Gather the other nobles. We need to be on hand to greet them," she forced herself to say.

Moments later, she stood outside her home with Mael, Judoc, and the other nobles as the Romans marched into the village. She made herself remain still, though fury burned within her at the sight of Catus, riding ahead of his personal military guard of soldiers.

His eyes were hard as he dismounted, approaching them.

"We have received word that the client king, Prasutagus, is dead," Catus said. He addressed the male nobles as he spoke, ignoring her. "You are now Roman subjects at the behest of Emperor Nero. These lands are the official property of the empire. Therefore, we are calling in the balance of the loans owed to us by your tribe. While we take inventory of the lands and property that will be seized, you and the other villagers are to be relocated to a location of our choosing. You have a fortnight to gather your possessions."

Shock coursed through her at his words, and she froze. Around her, the nobles murmured in horror and astonishment.

"My husband left these lands to our daughters in his will," she said, emerging from her shock to step forward, willing herself to remain calm. "I'm ruler of this tribe until they come of age."

"The Empire does not honor female succession," Catus said, his eyes straying to hers, filled with hot contempt. "As there is no male heir, these lands now belong to Emperor Nero."

"The chief's will is tribal law," Boudica hissed, her temper rising. "And you will address me; I'm the chieftain of this tribe. It's our right to obey the will of the former chieftain."

Catus's mouth tightened, and he glared at her as if she were a pesky rodent. He turned and signaled to his soldiers. They moved into offensive stances, their hands lowering to the hilts of their swords.

Judoc and the nobles surrounded her in a protective flank. Boudica returned Catus's glare, defiance filling every part of her. Around them, the villagers were taking notice of the conflict, and many were gathering around to watch.

"The sentence for disobeying an order from your

emperor is death," Catus snarled, giving the nobles who stood around her dark looks. "Now. Do you follow the whims of this foolish woman or do you submit to his order?"

Boudica ached for her sword—for any weapon. Rage had grabbed a hold of her, seizing her by the throat: hot, tight, and vicious. But she remained still, even as a burning tension strained the silence.

Catus stepped forward. He reminded Boudica of a spoiled child, his face crimson with fury. She'd seen the same look on her daughters' faces when they were mere babes and she'd refused them their favorite toy.

But Catus's childish fury abruptly vanished, and a cold, cruel smile curved his lips.

"Very well," he said, keeping his eyes on her, even as he addressed his soldiers. "Hand me the barbarian bitch."

14

Boudica stiffened, horror swirling throughout her veins, as Catus continued, "And locate her daughters. My men have been without the company of women for too long. They especially prefer virgins."

Shock rendered her still. She dimly heard the nobles let out a cry of outrage. She found that she could not move as Judoc attempted to shield her from Catus's soldiers, but they shoved him out of the way, and two soldiers gripped her arms, dragging her toward the village square. It was only then that she began to struggle as chaos descended around her.

Judoc and the nobles charged toward the Romans, but Catus's men subdued them. Startled villagers scrambled out of their homes and stopped tending to their fields as the Romans fanned out around the village, barring anyone who would try to interven.

Boudica's struggles were useless against the two soldiers who continued to drag her to the center of the square, binding her to a stake erected there. But Boudica's concern wasn't for herself. Panic rose in her chest as she saw several soldiers rushing toward Kensa's home.

Everything else around her faded away, and she let out a primal scream. They were looking for her daughters. Catus's words reverberated in her mind. *My men have been without the company of women for too long.*

"No!" she cried, anguish searing every part of her. "Please..."

Several male villagers, including Elouan, rushed toward Kensa's home, attempting to stop the soldiers, but one soldier, a tall muscular man with a jagged scar running down his jaw, stabbed one villager straight through with his sword, holding off the others as the remaining soldiers entered Kensa's home.

"No! Please! Please..." Boudica screamed.

Never in her life had she begged. Never had she thought she would beg a Roman for anything. But for her daughters she would do anything. She met Catus's eyes as he approached, her own eyes wild and pleading.

"Take my life," she whimpered. "Just do not harm my daughters. *Please!*"

But Catus only looked amused by her pleas, taking a flogger handed to him by a hovering soldier.

He stepped closer as she continued to struggle against her binds.

"Please . . ." she whispered. "Please . . . not my girls."

Catus backhanded her across the face. Her head flew back, her face stinging from the blow. But the physical pain was nothing. She could only think of her girls, her Brighid and Nolwenn.

Please, she prayed to the gods. *Please, not my daughters.*

"Let this be a warning to you all," Catus bellowed, turning to face the villagers who'd gathered round, held at bay by his soldiers. "As subjects of the Roman Empire, you must obey our orders. Regardless of your station."

Catus's words barely permeated Boudica's haze of panic as she heard her daughters' screams from Kensa's home.

"Please—mercy for my girls—mercy—" she wept.

Ignoring her cries, Catus stepped forward and stripped her of her cloak and tunic. She was naked, bared before all the villagers and the Romans. But she did not care. Her whole world was her daughters —their screams.

Gods, Boudica prayed. *Gods, no.*

Catus leaned in close to her ear, intimately close.

"Listen to the screams of your girls. Listen."

The screams of her daughters rose. An aching despair twisted inside her, more painful than any blow that could ever strike her. She sagged against the post, her sobs wracking her body.

"This is all because of your insolence, you foolish bitch. I will take great pleasure in this," Catus hissed.

He stepped back. Boudica was only dimly aware of his flogger striking the flesh of her back. Once. Twice. Three times. It struck her skin with such force that her flesh tore, and blood spilled down her back in rivulets. But Boudica felt nothing. She could only hear her daughters' continued screams.

"Please," she whispered, continuing to plead for them, even as Catus's flogger lashed, bruised and tore at her flesh. "Please . . ."

The pain from her torn flesh suddenly hit her, overwhelming her senses, even as she tried to ignore it, even as she tried to hold on to consciousness, to keep pleading for her daughters, but her world soon dissolved into a swirl of blackness.

WHEN BOUDICA OPENED HER EYES, SHE WAS BACK in her home on her bed of animal furs. Kensa hovered above her, her face bereft, along with two healers, who placed a salve of crushed arnica flowers to her broken skin.

For a moment, disorientation swirled through her, and then confusion, before the horrible events of the day came crashing back. Boudica sat up, crying out at the pain that shot through her.

"Boudica, your wounds," Kensa whispered, her voice breaking. "Lie back down, and—"

But Boudica ignored her, wincing against the pain, the still bleeding wounds on her back as she stumbled to her feet, her mind filled with the memory of her children's screams.

"The girls," she whispered, looking at Kensa.

"They're in my home; healers are tending to them. But Boudica, you shouldn't—"

Boudica ignored her, stumbling out of the door and making her way across the village to Kensa's home. She felt the eyes of the villagers on her, heard their horrified murmurings at the sight of their beaten and bruised leader, but Boudica was only focused on getting to her daughters.

She froze when she reached the doorway of Kensa's home. Brighid and Nolwenn lay on their beds while two female healers washed them and sang soft healing prayers.

Boudica pressed her hand to her mouth to stifle her cry of grief and rage at the sight. Her daughters, usually so joyful and full of life, were pale and bruised, staring straight ahead at nothing, the light gone from their eyes.

Boudica stumbled inside and sank to her knees between them, waving the healers away. Nolwenn didn't acknowledge her, while Brighid turned to face her. When she spoke, her voice was strangled and weak.

"Mama. I tried to fight them . . ."

Brighid dissolved into tears. Unable to contain her grief, Boudica pulled both her daughters into her arms, weeping as she rocked them.

"I'm here, my loves," she whispered into their hair. "Mama is sorry. Mama will protect you."

She stayed with them throughout the night, rocking and singing to them, just as she had when they were still babes. Even after their fatigue claimed them, she didn't move from their sides.

When her own tears subsided, she gazed down at their sleeping faces, and a different emotion arose from the ashes of her grief.

Rage. The thirst for vengeance. The rage that filled her after Antedios and Prasutagus's deaths was but a shadow of the rage she felt now. In both those instances, she'd ignored it, forcing herself to quell her fury.

But there would be no more quelling her rage. She allowed it to coil around her body, to hold her firmly in its grip. Her father was dead, there was no need to play the dutiful daughter. Her husband was dead, there was no need to play the dutiful wife. She was leader of the tribe now. Chieftain. Queen. The Romans had taken much from her; she would allow them to take no more. The time for grief and despair had passed.

Now was the time for vengeance.

She recalled her father's words from long ago. They rang clear in her ears now, as clear as the war cries the tribal warriors bellowed before leaping into battle.

That rage that's scorching your insides like fire? When the time is right, use it to your advantage. It is best to know when to fight, girl. When to win.

That time was now. She would take her revenge on Catus and the men who'd violated her daughters. But she would not stop there.

She would expel the murderous, treacherous Romans from their lands.

III

60 CE

The Warrior Queen

15

At first light the next morning, Boudica entered the meeting hall with her shoulders squared and her head held erect, the way she'd seen her father carry himself when he presided over meetings with the nobles. Her face still bore the bruise of Catus's blow, and her back screamed with pain from the wounds that crisscrossed her back, wounds the healers had tried to salve with elderberries. Yet she held on to the sensation of pain; it was a reminder of what the Romans had done.

The men gathered in the meeting hall were not just the nobles of her tribe; they were also the nobles of a neighboring tribe, the Trinovantes.

The night before, she'd sent for Mael and told him what she planned to do. She'd braced herself for words of caution and protest, but he'd not looked surprised.

"This day was a long time coming," he'd said simply.

"We need greater numbers if we're to fight. I want to send a messenger to other tribes—the Trinovantes, the Cantiaci, Durotriges, and the Belgae."

Though her tribe had been enemies to these tribes at various points in the past, they'd all suffered at the hands of the Romans, and the Durotriges had rebelled against them most recently.

"I also want to send a messenger to the Brigantes tribe in the north."

Only then had Mael gone still and given her a disapproving frown. The Brigantes and their queen, Cartimandua, were long-time allies of Rome. She'd heard her father and nobles speak ill of the northern tribe when she was young. But alliances could be broken, and she'd heard tales of how strong the Brigantes warriors were. And the Brigantes had rebelled against Rome in the past. There was a part of her that hoped Cartimandua would have sympathy for a fellow female ruler, one of the few in these lands, one who'd been so violently wronged by the Romans.

"Their queen is loyal to Rome. There are even rumors that she and the new governor are lovers."

"If we are to have victory, we need every man willing to fight," she'd firmly returned.

Mael had given her a terse nod and reluctantly agreed to send a messenger north.

The Trinovantes nobles, being the closest in distance to the Iceni, had come quickly after receiving her message. She prayed the other tribes would join as they began their march to the Roman settlements, increasing the size of their army.

Now, Boudica took in the chieftain of the Trinovantes: Cadell, a tall man who appeared to be in his thirtieth year. He reminded Boudica of a wolf with his sharp blue eyes and burnished blond hair, his skin covered from head to toe with tribal tattoos signifying his status as chieftain.

In years past, her tribe had warred with the Trinovantes over land and resources. They'd not fought with them for some time, and she prayed they could put any lingering hostilities aside to focus on their common enemy.

All eyes were on her as she made her way to the head of the hall, trailed by Mael. Though none of the nobles spoke a word, she could see shock in their eyes at her bruised appearance.

Good, she thought. She wanted them to see what their Roman "allies" were capable of.

When she reached the head of the hall, she turned to face them. There would be no preamble to her words; she would get straight to the matter at hand. There was no time to waste.

"I called you here for our tribes to unite. I want us to rise against Rome. Expel them from our lands for good."

The silence that followed her words seemed to stretch for an eternity before the hall erupted into cries of dismay and disbelief—mainly from the Trinovantes.

Cadell finally stepped forward, gesturing to his men for silence.

"We know what happened here today," he said, his gaze lingering on Boudica's bruised face, "and it's an outrage. But my tribe's lived in peace for years under the rule of the Romans."

"How long do you think that will last?" Boudica challenged. She'd prepared herself for counterarguments such as these. "Catus and his men are returning to take our lands and make us their slaves. If you think they'll stop with just our tribe, just our lands—you're a fool."

The Trinovantes nobles rumbled in protest at the insult, but Cadell didn't seem perturbed, furrowing his brow as he considered her words.

"Our healers scented traces of poison from the henbane plant on my husband's breath," Boudica said, anger spiraling in her gut at the memory. The nobles stiffened at her words, their eyes filling with rage and horror.

"Poison's the coward's way of killing," Boudica continued, over their rumbles of anger. "The Roman way. You all knew Chieftain Prasutagus. He was a good man and only wanted peace. He did everything the Romans asked. He didn't deserve such a death. And—my daughters—"

Her voice wavered, and the anguish that seized

her rendered her silent for a moment, as the memory of their screams resounded in her ears.

"But this—this isn't about what the Romans have done to my family," she said, forcing herself to continue. "It's about us all. They've taken our weapons. Starved us with their taxes on our grain. Conscripted our sons, husbands, fathers and brothers to die in their armies."

The nobles fell silent. She took in their tight, furious expressions; her words were landing.

"We've no choice but to fight back. I know it in my bones—as do all of you. This day was bound to come. I know I'm but a woman," she said, pulling herself to her full height, a height that towered over many of the men. She knew what they were all thinking; it was rare to follow a woman into battle, and she doubted any of them had ever taken command from one. Though their tribes had some female warriors, female chieftains weren't common. "But the blood of Chieftain Antedios runs in my veins. I was the daughter of a great chieftain, wife to another. My father once rose against them. I will finish his fight."

The nobles remained silent for such a long moment that defeat settled over her. If she couldn't rouse the others to fight—

But the crowd before her parted. Judoc emerged, sinking to his knees before her.

"Your father saved my life many times in battle. In his name—and our tribe's name—I'll fight with you," Judoc said. His eyes darkened, and he continued, "I've always wanted to rip the armor from the Roman cowards and kill 'em with my bare hands. Show them how a real man fights."

Boudica smiled, giving him a grateful nod. Hope coursed through her as one by one, more Icenian nobles joined her side, pledging their desire and promise to fight the Romans.

When the nobles of her tribe stood gathered around her, she met the eyes of Cadell and the Trinovantes nobles who surrounded him. They still looked uncertain.

"The Romans will not stop with us," Boudica said, her voice rising with urgency. "Your lands neighbor ours. It's only a matter of time before they extend their reach. You know this to be true. We're stronger if we band together to fight them."

Her words propelled the nobles into action, and they stepped forward to join her, giving her respectful nods as they did. Soon, all of the Trinovantes nobles had joined her side. All except for one.

Cadell. He remained where he was, studying her with a look of wary caution.

"You're not the first to rise against them. You mentioned your father. Look at what happened to him."

"All the more reason to finish what he started," Boudica returned, trying not to flinch at the memory of her father's dead, still body in his chariot.

"If we stand against them, there will be no

coming back from this," Cadell continued. "Not this time. Their vengeance will be—"

"No worse than what we suffer now," Boudica interrupted. "They've already taken everything from us. We've nothing more to lose."

Cadell continued to survey her, and she detected a flicker of grudging respect in his eyes. He stepped forward, bowing his head low.

"Then we rise against them," he said.

At his words, the nobles around them bellowed tribal war cries. Relief flowed through her, along with stirrings of hope, emerging from the darkness that had dominated her mind since Catus's attack.

Later, after they'd discussed preliminary plans for their attack, Boudica slipped out of the meeting hall, telling the others she would shortly return.

She made her way into the surrounding woodlands until she reached the same clearing where she'd fought with Prasutagus in her youth. She sank down in the center of the clearing, closing her eyes.

Her promise to Prasutagus to not seek revenge had been in the back of her mind ever since she decided to fight. Her guilt now rose in her chest, as sharp as a sword's blade piercing the skin.

"My love. My husband," she whispered. "I do what I must. For our daughters. For your memory. For our people. Forgive me."

The breeze rustling through the trees was her only answer, and she stood, allowing her resolve to will away the remaining guilt that filled her. There was no time for regret now.

She left the clearing to rejoin her men.

Boudica watched as Mael scrawled a rough makeshift map of their tribal lands with a stick, along with the surrounding lands on the dirt floor of the meeting hall.

It was the next morning, and Boudica stood gathered with Mael, Cadell and Judoc. The nobles from both tribes were scattered around the meeting hall, talking amongst themselves.

After the nobles agreed to fight the Romans, Boudica held a meeting for the villagers the next day, informing them of the upcoming battle. She'd prepared for refusals and pleas for peace, but the villagers had bellowed cries of agreement, many even volunteering to join the fight, and Boudica's heart had swelled with pride.

The mood of the villagers shifted following her announcement. Their grief over the beloved chieftain's death and the outrage his wife and daughters had suffered at the hands of the Romans seemed to vanish, and a new sentiment had arisen, one which had dimmed during the alliance with the Romans. Defiance. She heard it in the tribal cries the villagers bellowed when she announced they would rise against Rome, she saw it in the fierce determination in the eyes of every villager—men and women, the young and the old. It was a remnant of the fierce warrior culture that sustained the Iceni before their acquiescence to the Romans, a fiery defiance that swelled once more. Catus and his men had destroyed the uneasy peace that existed between her tribe and Rome. The anger that Boudica had quelled for so many years was now unleashed not just within her, but within the villagers as well.

"The governor, Suetonius Paulinus, is in Mona," Mael said, pulling Boudica from her thoughts. He used a stick to point to a region in the north. "That gives us time."

"Why is he in Mona?" Boudica asked with a sliver of unease. Mona was the sacred training ground of the druid priests.

"Our scouts tell us they are slaughtering the priests," Mael said. His expression remained stoic, though his voice wavered.

"What?" Boudica breathed, a rush of rage filling her chest. "Why wasn't I told of this?"

"Because there is nothing you could have done," Mael said. "I only learned of it after the Romans marched north."

"Why are they attacking our priests?" Boudica demanded.

"The Romans believe the druids incite rebellions among the tribes." A ghost of a sad, weary smile appeared on Mael's face. "They are right."

Boudica closed her eyes, clenching her trembling

hands at her sides. It was true; she'd overheard her father and the nobles speak of how the druids urged many tribes to resist the Romans, ever since they first invaded.

"We must focus on what is at hand," Mael said, sensing Boudica's anger. "And that is striking while the Roman governor is away."

"If the governor is away . . . the gods favor us," Cadell said, his eyes gleaming.

"They slaughter our holy men," Judoc growled, glaring at him. "And you say the gods favor us?"

"It gives us time. He's taken much of the Roman army with him. We need to move quickly," Cadell said firmly.

Judoc continued to glower at him; Boudica noticed with unease that he'd clenched his hands into fists at his sides. She'd learned that Judoc's father and grandfather had both died in battle serving previous chieftains, and he was raised by his brother to become the same: a deeply loyal warrior. From the many combat challenges she'd seen Judoc win over the years, she knew that he was fierce in one-on-one combat—and that he had a blazing temper.

But Judoc's loyalty to Boudica and their tribe wouldn't allow him to fight Cadell if she forbade it.

"Cadell is right. This does give us a chance," she said, leveling Judoc with a look of warning.

Judoc's face tightened, but he gave her a respectful nod.

"What of Catus? And his men?" she asked, trying

to keep her voice steady as she thought of the man who'd flogged her and ordered the rape of her daughters.

"The scouts tell us he's at a trading post; the Romans call it Londinium," Mael said.

"Then we march there first," Boudica said, a dark thrill rippling through her as she imagined subjecting Catus to a long and painful death.

"No. That shouldn't be our first battle," Cadell interjected.

"Why is that?" Judoc snapped.

"The nearest Roman settlement is Camulodunum. It's more important to the Romans. It's their capital, where their governor resides. And," he continued, pointing at an area on Mael's scrawled map, "it's closer. Less than a day's march. Only retired soldiers and nonfighting folk live there. It's easier to attack."

"Camulodunum was the dwelling of your tribe before the Romans came," Judoc said, his eyes narrowing with suspicion. "We're not fighting to reclaim your old lands."

"That's not why I want us to march there first," Cadell bit out. He turned his attention to Boudica. "I know you want Catus. But you must understand—Catus is a coward. He'll flee Londinium if he knows a large army's coming for him."

"You don't know that," Judoc interrupted, advancing toward Cadell. "If Boudica wants to go to Londinium first, then—"

"I was addressing Boudica, not her guard," Cadell snapped, taking a step toward him. "As chieftain of my tribe, I know—"

"You're not my chieftain," Judoc snarled.

The meeting hall had fallen silent, and the nobles of both tribes glanced their way. Boudica noticed with unease that Cadell's men had frozen as if preparing themselves to defend their chieftain.

She moved between Cadell and Judoc, keeping her focus on Judoc.

"Judoc," she said firmly. "Now is not the time."

Judoc remained tense, and she feared he would step around her and attack Cadell. But he stepped back, though he kept a hot glare trained on the other man.

Cadell turned his focus to her, along with the other nobles. As the one who'd called for the uprising, it was up to her to decide on where to march first. Her heart hammered in her chest as the full weight of her newfound leadership settled on her shoulders like a great weight. For a moment, she wished that her father was here to give her guidance.

She took a breath, her heart hardening with resolve before turning to Mael.

"We'll take them by surprise. Camulodunum is closer; we'll march there first."

"Good," Cadell said, looking pleased by her decision, while Judoc scowled. "But the Romans will not think of a woman as a threat."

Boudica stiffened, anger prickling her chest.

Judoc's expression filled with fury at Cadell's words, even Mael looked taken aback. But she spoke up before either of them could speak, not wanting the tension to spike once more.

"I know."

"I'm not saying it to insult you," Cadell assured her. "I believe you can use their doubt to your benefit. We can have our scouts spread a rumor for the Roman scouts. A false one."

Boudica considered his words.

"We can say that none of my tribesmen would follow a woman into battle," she said slowly.

"And that you could only raise a small army of women," Mael added.

"Yes. Let them think we can be easily defeated," Cadell said.

Mael stepped forward, placing his hands on her shoulders, fire in his eyes.

"And then you prove them wrong."

16

In the days before a battle, the atmosphere in the village was often festive, with the warriors spending their nights in the chieftain's home feasting, drinking, and engaging in combat challenges. When Boudica was still a girl, she would lay awake at night listening to the festivities with envy, wishing that she was going to battle with them.

But for the upcoming battle, Boudica held no celebratory feast. This was no mere conflict with another tribe for territory; this battle was for their very freedom.

The night before they were to march, Boudica and the other warriors went out to a sacred grove with Mael and several other priests to receive blessings from the gods before battle. As she knelt before Mael, her eyes closed as he smeared the blood of a hare on her cheeks and forehead, she prayed for strength, for the ability to set aside the trepidation that had coiled in her belly at the thought of what lay ahead.

"When I was a boy, my brother would put me on his shoulders to watch the warriors fight in battle," Judoc told her, after the prayers concluded and the warriors filed out of the grove. "As they charged into battle, they'd scream and bellow prayers to the gods for victory. It was a beautiful sight. More beautiful than any woman I've ever seen. I've dreamed about going into battle. It's the only time I truly feel alive."

"But . . . you've been to battle before," Boudica said.

"It only truly feels like battle when I fight against the invaders. I never trusted the Romans, not even when your father bent the knee. That first rebellion he led may have failed, but I'm glad you're continuing his fight. I look forward to killing the Roman bastards."

Boudica smiled. Judoc encompassed everything she'd always admired about the tribal warriors: the bravery that bordered on recklessness, the eagerness to protect the tribe, to fight for them all.

"Thank you," she said. "For being the first man to come forward when I asked."

"It was my duty," he said simply. "You're the chieftain now. I follow my chief."

He left her behind with a respectful bow of his head, and she watched him go, heart hammering as the weight of his words sank in. *You're the chieftain now.*

She barely slept that night, curled around her daughters in her large bed of furs, where they'd all slept since the day of Catus's attack. She'd sat them down to tell them she was leading the tribe into battle; Nolwenn had reacted with fearful tears, Brighid with an unnerving silence. She'd assured them she was leading this fight for them and for her people, but the girls hadn't seemed at all reassured.

She gazed down at their sleeping forms, reaching out to stroke their hair. They were not the same since the attack; the healers told her their physical wounds would soon heal, but it was their hearts and minds that concerned Boudica. She would remember every detail of Catus's attack for the rest of her days, from the crimson of the Roman soldiers' cloaks, the feel of the flogger's sting against her skin, to the sound of her daughters' screams. But she wanted that day to fade from her daughters' memories as soon as possible, and prayed for the quick passage of time, the only thing that could dull such a dark and violent memory.

She managed to drift off into a restless sleep, awaking just as sunlight filtered into their home.

As Boudica's attendants entered to help her prepare for battle, Kensa came to take the girls to her home, carrying their still sleeping bodies out with another attendant.

Boudica watched them go, her pulse fluttering wildly as one attendant painted blue war paint onto her face and arms, in the design of the tribal tattoos every warrior wore to battle. A second attendant wound her hair into several long braids before placing the royal chieftain's torc around her neck.

Boudica tried to calm herself, but her heart continued to race and her hands shook at her sides. She always thought excitement would fill her when she fought her first battle, yet now she only felt fear, dread that tightened around her throat like the hands of an invisible foe. She had to admit to herself with grudging reluctance that the Romans were formidable; even her father had bent the knee to them once. What if she didn't survive the first battle? What if they overtook her army and slaughtered them before they even had a chance to fight?

Her attendants stepped back, and she tried to force aside her worried thoughts as one handed her a mirror. She took in her appearance. War paint and intricate tribal tattoos covered every part of her flesh, and her green eyes shone bright and fierce like a wolf's deadly gaze. She looked every inch the fierce tribal warrior.

But inside, she felt like a frightened girl.

The mirror trembled in her grasp. She lowered it, nodding her thanks.

"Mama?"

Boudica whirled to face the doorway. Kensa had returned with her daughters, who stared at her with wide-eyed astonishment; this was the first time they'd seen her dressed as a warrior.

"They woke up as soon as I settled them into their beds," Kensa said with an apologetic smile.

Brighid and Nolwenn approached Boudica tentatively as if she were a dangerous animal. Boudica smiled to soften her intimidating appearance, kneeling down to their level. Once Nolwenn drew near, she reached out to touch Boudica's face, some of her war paint transferring to her small fingers.

Brighid didn't look as awestruck as her sister, and defiance shone in her gaze.

"I want to fight," she said.

Boudica stilled, pride and heartbreak washing over her. Her Brighid was so much like her when she was a girl. She reached out to cup Brighid's face, gazing into the green eyes that mirrored her own. Is this what she'd looked like when she came to her father as a child, begging to fight with the warriors?

"You're just a child, Brighid. You'll be with the other families watching the battle; this isn't your fight. I—I should've protected the both of you," she continued, her voice wavering. She reached out to cup Nolwenn's face as well, her expression turning fierce. "As long as I breathe, no one will ever harm either of you again."

Brighid's eyes narrowed with anger, and she turned to storm away. Boudica called after her, but she quickly disappeared out the door.

"Give her time," Kensa said gently, before kneeling down next to Nolwenn. "Tell your mama goodbye."

Nolwenn obeyed, flinging her arms around Boudica's neck. Boudica held onto her daughter tight, whispering words of love. When Nolwenn pulled back, her brown eyes were wet with tears.

"I'll comfort Brighid," Nolwenn said, wiping her tears away. "She doesn't like to show it when she's hurt."

"I know, my love," Boudica murmured, her heart clenching at Nolwenn's innate compassion.

"Are—are you going to join the gods like Papa?" Nolwenn asked, her voice small and wavering. "That's what can happen when warriors go to battle. They join the gods."

"No," Boudica said fiercely, though the same fear had haunted her, that she would die in battle and leave her daughters alone. "I will return to you. I promise."

"I want to say my own goodbye," Kensa said, after an attendant led Nolwenn away. She took Boudica's hands, giving her a wavering smile. "When you were a girl . . . remember when you spilled your father's war paint all over yourself? Rozen was furious."

"My skin was tinged blue for days," Boudica murmured, shaking her head at the memory. "You and Prasutagus kept teasing me."

"You were so small. You looked a fool."

Boudica's smile faded as she looked down at her shaking hands, shame coursing through her.

"I've wanted to be a warrior for most of my life. And now that I must fight . . . I'm frightened."

Her shame swelled; she hadn't wanted to admit her fear to anyone.

"Remember what Rozen used to tell us? 'Fear shows strength,'" Kensa said, squeezing her hands. "It's your first battle; of course you're afraid. But you have your people behind you, an army that stands with you. Elouan's fighting in this battle; if there were anyone else leading this army I'd fear for him. But I don't have fear with you as the leader. Boudica . . . you were never like the rest of the women of the tribe. I always knew you were meant for something . . . greater."

Kensa's brown eyes glistened with tears, and a rush of emotion filled Boudica.

"*This* is what you were meant for," Kensa continued. "To fight. For all of us. Now go. Our people are waiting for you."

When Boudica left the chieftain's home, Judoc and several warriors who would serve as her guards waited for her. They flanked her as she mounted her horse, before hopping astride their own horses.

Boudica rode her horse to the square at a slow trot, trying to still her shaking hands. In the village square, a massive army of Iceni and Trinovantes were gathered, their number so great that they spilled out from the village square and into the surrounding countryside: men—and some women—from all trades. There were warriors, farmers, craftsmen, blacksmiths. Many of them carried hunting spears and household weapons, others carried swords and javelins. Their families were gathered in the rear of the army: some on foot, others crowded into wagons and chariots.

Cadell and other high-ranking warriors sat astride their horses at the head of the square. All eyes were on her; she prayed they didn't notice her shaking hands.

At the sight of her, the army whooped out tribal war cries, working themselves into the customary frenzy before battle. Soon, the tribal cries ceased, all eyes still trained on her, and she realized they wanted her to speak. She tried to think of what her father would say, with his booming voice that could sway thousands.

A hush fell as the army waited. She closed her eyes, expelling a breath. She would start with her father's words, but the next words she spoke would have to be all her own.

She thought of her father's still body, Prasutagus dying in her arms, her daughters' screams, the flogger whipping her skin. And her rage quelled her fear.

"My father the chieftain once told me that it's best to know when to fight. Now is that time."

The ground seemed to shake from the ferocious shouts and battle cries from the crowd. Bolstered by the reaction, Boudica continued, her voice rising above their cries, "We have bowed down to the Romans for too long. They have taken our lands, violated and murdered us, used us for their own gain. But no more. We will fight for the lands gifted to us from the gods. We will fight to live and breathe as free men!"

The army roared with triumph. She met Mael's eyes, who stood to the side of the massive army. He gave her a brief nod, and she saw a glimmer of pride in his expression.

As the cries of the crowd grew in intensity, Boudica gripped the reins of her horse, guiding him out of the square and away from the village, her heart thundering with the hope of victory.

17

It's quiet, Aelius thought, a chill creeping down his spine. *It's too quiet.*

He stood on the outskirts of the Roman colonia of Camulodunum. The colonia, with its paved streets of gravel, dotted with red-tiled roofs of white buildings, was usually populated with citizens going about their day and native farmers toiling the surrounding fields.

His gaze strayed to the temple dedicated to the Emperor Claudius that dominated the central square; at this time children would circle around it, giggling and chasing each other.

But now, even with the infantry of two hundred Roman auxiliary troops who swarmed through the streets, taking up guard at various posts, and the upper-class residents who packed their horses and carts to leave, it was still quiet. An eerie, unsettling hush had settled over the streets.

Aelius turned, watching the residents who remained barricade themselves inside their homes. Other residents streamed into the main temple for refuge, directed by retired Roman soldiers who also resided in Camulodunum.

Aelius stiffened as a young soldier, Nicon, came to join him at his post. This was the first campaign Aelius had undertaken with Nicon, and he disliked the younger soldier; he was brash and arrogant. As far as Aelius knew, Nicon had not yet fought in a single battle, yet he acted as if he were Caesar himself.

"The residents are leaving only as a precaution," Nicon said with a dismissive wave of his hand. "These barbarians keep trying to rise against us, and we defeat them every time."

Aelius chose not to respond. He and the other soldiers had received word from scouts that two southern tribes planned to attack Camulodunum. With Governor Paulinus away on a campaign, Catus had provided a small detachment of soldiers to defend the colonia from the barbarian army. He didn't know much about the tribes who were rebelling, other than that they'd previously been Roman allies. He'd heard conflicting rumors about the army itself; a pervasive one contended that it was a small army led by women, easy to defeat.

Aelius's eye caught the statue of the goddess Victory, perched in the central square, as it tottered in the light breeze. He froze when it tumbled over and shattered into many pieces on the ground. Panic coursed through him; such an occurrence was an ill omen.

He turned to Nicon, but the young soldier's attentions were trained behind him, on two pretty young women who climbed into their father's wagon. They blushed when he met their eyes.

"Nicon—" he began, wanting to warn him of the ill omen, but stopped when he heard something that sounded like thunder. He looked up at the sky, but it remained a clear and pristine blue.

Aelius tensed as the noise became more clear. It was the sound of pounding horse hooves and war cries. He turned. In the distance, he saw a massive army surging toward Camulodunum like an unstoppable avalanche.

At his side, Nicon went still, the color draining from his face. Aelius swallowed as he looked around at the other dumbfounded soldiers stationed at their posts. None of them had expected an army of this size; the scouts had told them the barbarian army numbered in the low hundreds.

"We must retreat—their numbers are too great!" Aelius shouted, loud enough for the other soldiers to hear. "Quickly!"

Nicon nodded his agreement. But as he turned to flee, he abruptly stiffened. Aelius stumbled back, his heart leaping into his throat. A barbarian had hurled a hunting spear straight into Nicon's back. Aelius watched in dazed shock as Nicon slumped to the ground, dead.

A barrage of arrows fell onto the streets of Camulodunum like a swarm of locusts. Aelius, along with the other soldiers around him, scrambled into protective positions beneath their shields

Gods protect us, Aelius prayed, thinking of the wife he'd left behind in Rome, of their young daughter. *Gods have mercy on us all.*

BOUDICA KEPT HER GAZE FOCUSED ON THE RED-tiled roofs of Camulodunum as her army surged toward it. She'd never ventured far from her village; the farthest she'd ever gone was to the outskirts of the Trinovantes lands, when she'd watched her tribe battle against them as a girl. She'd tried to imagine what the rest of the lands the Romans called Brittania looked like. Was it dominated by trees, like the lands around her village? Or was it a mass of rolling hills? Were other villages like hers, with Roman-style buildings sprinkled throughout, or did thatch-roofed, native-style homes and buildings dominate?

But the lands and villages of Britannia varied. During their ride south, they'd passed massive swaths of green fields with patches of forests in the distance; multiple streams and rivers that weaved through the lands like forest snakes. The villages they passed, some small, some large, were dotted with roundhouses and farmsteads, some with Roman buildings, others with none at all, and both tribal and Roman roads crisscrossed the lands.

With each village they passed, villagers stepped out of their homes or farmsteads, watching in awe as the army marched by. Some, she noticed with a swelling of pride, grabbed their household weapons to join.

As the army drew closer to their destination, Boudica's nervousness had returned. Cadell, who rode at her side, had seemed to sense it.

"I was in my eleventh year when my father sent me to my first battle," he'd told her. "I wept like a babe the night before."

"I've fought before," Boudica had returned, keeping her voice steady. She couldn't show fear, not as leader of the army. "I first used a sword my seventh year."

"Tribal mock battles and practice fights—they're not the same as true battle," Cadell had said. "They're not the same as killing a man."

"I'll have no trouble killing Romans."

"Watching the life leave a man's eyes by the thrust of your weapon—it's something the bravest warrior never gets used to. When the time comes to take your first life . . . just remember what you're fighting for."

It was these words that filled Boudica's thoughts as her army descended upon Camulodunum. She whispered a quick prayer to Andraste as she leapt from her horse, taking out her sword and charging into the Roman capital with the other warriors.

Amid the sea of fighters, the Roman soldiers darted forward, but they were quickly overwhelmed by her army. Boudica evaded the swing of a soldier's sword as he swung at her. All her years of training with Prasutagus, of watching the combat challenges like a hawk came through, and it was like a dark dance as the soldier again lunged toward her, this time nearly stabbing her straight through. She recalled her father's warning to her that fateful night years ago, of not being too rash, of practicing patience. She held back, waiting for the soldier to again lunge for her, and whirled to jut her sword forward, spearing it into the flesh of his throat.

His eyes met hers, wide and startled, the blood that seeped from his wound as red as his cloak before he crumpled to the ground.

For a moment, everything around Boudica stilled as she gazed down at the dead soldier, at the blood on her sword. It was the first time she'd killed anyone. For all her childhood dreams of being a warrior, she'd never so much as killed an animal. She stood there, gazing down at him for a moment, and any guilt she might have felt, any sliver of remorse faded when she thought of her father's dead body; Prasutagus's feverish face as he lay dying, her girls' screams as the Roman soldiers violated them.

She charged forward with the same roar that the warriors around her bellowed, darting past Judoc, as he strangled a Roman soldier with his bare hands, and Cadell, who moved with the ease of a seasoned warrior, slashing down several soldiers with his sword.

Her movements were quick and frenetic as she fought more Roman soldiers, her blade sinking into their throats or through any bare piece of flesh she could strike. She evaded their attacks with relative ease, and the entire world around her faded as each soldier she cut down led to less, and when she looked up some time later, her face splattered with blood, she realized that they'd overrun the capital; there were only a few Roman soldiers remaining, and tribal warriors now surrounded them.

Judoc approached her through the crowd, holding a lit torch. He gestured toward the buildings, his expression solemn.

"You should be the one to do it."

She looked around; the warriors were all looking at her. Many were bruised and covered with blood, but there was fire in their eyes.

Taking the torch, she moved toward the first row of Roman buildings that faced her, hatred searing through her at the sight. They were a symbol of Rome's usurping of their lands. She tossed the torch onto the roof of the first building; one of a series of workshops and store rooms. The fire caught on quickly, spreading to the rest of the buildings.

Boudica turned, gesturing to the other warriors to continue what she'd started. They charged forward with torches of their own, setting the main buildings on fire.

She moved through the streets, past the mass of fighters who'd knocked down the statue of Emperor Claudius in the central square, hacking away at it with their weapons.

But her focus was centered on the temple just beyond the statue. A group of fighters surrounded it, trying to hack their way inside with their weapons. Inside, the terrified whimpers and cries of the surviving Roman residents increased.

Boudica approached the temple, turning to face the fighters. Fury scorched her insides as she recalled how she'd pled for mercy from Catus, how she'd wept as his soldiers stole her daughters' innocence. How many other innocents had the Romans violated and killed?

"They cry for mercy," Boudica shouted. "How many times have we cried for mercy?!"

The fighters bellowed a chorus of outraged cries. Boudica raised her voice so that the cowards inside the temple could hear every word.

"We show them the same mercy they've shown us!"

As the fighters continued hacking their way into the temple, a firm hand clamped onto Boudica's shoulder, pulling her back from the temple. She turned to find Cadell standing behind her.

"A scout," he said, gesturing toward a man in the

square dismounting from his horse. "He brings news of the Romans."

Boudica approached the scout with Cadell, her heart thundering in her chest.

"What news?" she demanded.

"A Roman legion's coming from the west," he replied, his face pale. "They're not far. I counted two thousand."

BOUDICA HAD FORGOTTEN HOW SILENT THE forest was. How you could hear your breath over the faint whisper of leaves rustling in the wind, how your heartbeat could thunder in your ears with the mighty force of a drum.

She held her breath as she crouched behind the trunk of a large oak tree. She melded in with the surrounding greenery. Before leaving Camulodunum, an attendant had coated her face and arms in green war paint. She was one of hundreds of tribal warriors crouched behind trees in the silent forest, waiting for the Roman legion to cross their path.

Even with her thundering heartbeat, a swell of pride washed over her as she took in her fellow warriors. The Romans had underestimated the natives' knowledge of their lands, how well they knew every facet of the woodlands that dominated Britannia. She met Cadell's eyes across the grove; he and Judoc had insisted on coming with the contingent of men she'd brought with her to stop the Roman advance. They'd decided to surprise the Romans with a smaller contingent rather than having the whole army fight them at Camulodunum; she prayed to Andraste that the surprise attack would work.

She stiffened when she heard the clatter of approaching horse hooves and peered around the tree. In the near distance, she could see Quintus Cerealis, the Roman general, leading his soldiers down the paved Roman road that cut through the woodlands. His eyes, and the eyes of his soldiers, were trained only on the road before them, not on the surrounding trees, where their enemies lay in wait.

As soon as Quintus and his soldiers were in striking distance, Boudica signaled to Cadell. He turned to his men, giving them a nod, and the warriors leapt out from the trees, shouting tribal cries.

Boudica darted out with the warriors, and together they cut down the startled soldiers. Unlike before, there was no hesitation as she struck down soldiers with her sword. Killing that first Roman soldier in Camulodunum had unleashed something in her, something dark and lethal, something that had been growing within her for years.

She moved through the surge of fighting bodies around her, making her way toward Quintus, who fought off two warriors while still astride his horse.

Judoc caught her eye and hurried forward to hold the rearing animal still as she reached the startled Quintus. Judoc reached up to disarm him as

Boudica climbed onto the horse, meeting Quintus's terrified dark eyes. He braced himself, as if preparing for her to strike him down with her sword, and she ached to do it. But this was one Roman that she needed alive.

She leveled him with a hard stare as he opened his eyes, before addressing him in his tongue.

"Tell your Roman masters that if you do not leave our lands, we will kill every Roman man, woman and child that remains."

She held his gaze for a long moment, allowing her words to settle. She must have looked like a wild beast to him, with her raging eyes, the green paint covering her face and body splattered with blood. Quintus swallowed and gave her a jerky nod.

She leapt down from his horse, hitting its flank. Quintus tugged on the reins, turning his horse to flee, trampling over the bodies of his dead soldiers as he raced away.

"I think you frightened him," Judoc said, amusement lacing his tone as he came to stand next to her.

"Good. As long as he passes my message on to his masters," Boudica replied, watching Quintus ride away.

When they returned to Camulodunum, the day had grown dark. Its buildings now lay in ashes from the fires, and the temple was razed to the ground.

As Boudica entered the square on horseback, ahead of her contingent of men, scores of warriors approached her. She stilled as they all began to chant.

Their words were faint at first, but they soon grew into a powerful roar.

"Bou-di-ca! Bou-di-ca! Bou-di-ca!"

Boudica allowed herself to smile, but it wasn't for herself. It was for the renewed vigor and hope in the eyes of the warriors, men and women who'd been downtrodden by the Romans for too long.

She rode her horse forward, raising her voice to carry over their chants.

"This is not my victory. This is our victory!"

The chants turned into triumphant shouts and tribal cries, and hope swelled within her. They had won their first victory and were one step closer to ridding their lands of the Roman pestilence.

18

Boudica's army set up camp on the outskirts of the still burning Camulodunum, the air thick with the ash of burning buildings and bodies. The warriors celebrated their victory, drinking and feasting over various bonfires they'd set up around camp.

Boudica, Kensa, her daughters, and attendants were situated on the far edge of camp. She sat opposite her daughters, who were curled up on beds of animal pelts, drifting off to sleep. She reached out to gently touch Nolwenn's face. Nolwenn gave her a faint smile, her eyes fluttering shut. When Boudica tried to touch Brighid, she shrank back from her touch, turning her back to her. A shard of hurt pierced Boudica, but she forced a smile.

"Sleep well, little one," she murmured.

Brighid didn't respond.

Boudica got to her feet, moving toward their

bonfire. Kensa sat before it, warming her hands over the flames.

"Patience," Kensa murmured, jerking her head back to where Brighid lay. "She shows her pain with anger. She still needs—"

"Time," Boudica concluded. "I know."

"She was quiet today, but I could tell she was proud of you," Kensa said, giving her an encouraging smile. "We all were. I almost wept when I heard them chanting your name. Elouan told me the warriors are all invigorated now."

Boudica returned her smile, though the hope she'd felt earlier had faded to hollowness. There was a time when she'd dreamed of having her name chanted in reverence by fellow warriors, but that was when she was a foolish child. She wanted Prasutagus back, alive, more than she wanted glory. She wanted her daughters' innocence returned to them. She wanted the Romans gone from their lands.

"I keep thinking of the foolish girl I was," Kensa said, shaking her head with rueful regret. "Focused only on marrying Arthek and having his sons. None of that mattered, not with the Romans hovering in the shadows like wolves, on the verge of devouring everything. After Arthek died . . . I was jealous of you. You had what I'd always wanted. A husband who adored you. Two beautiful children. There were times when —when I wished they were mine," Kensa added, a guilty flush spreading across her cheeks. "And now, after all that's happened . . . I feel like my envy brought all this on you."

"You didn't know what was to come. No one did. You're not to blame for what has happened—only the Romans are," Boudica assured her.

"You seemed to know. You hated the Romans long before the rest of us did. Watching you today . . . you made me think of Andraste herself. It almost made me want to pick up a sword."

Boudica tried to think of the peaceful Kensa, who detested the sight of blood, brandishing a sword. Her lips twitched.

"What?" Kensa asked.

"I'm trying to think of you with a sword," Boudica said.

For a moment, a look of offense crossed Kensa's features, before her own lips twitched, and she chuckled.

They both laughed, and Boudica allowed her mirth to soothe her. After this day of fire and blood, she needed a moment like this. A moment to not think of all the blood that would be shed in the days to come.

WHEN BOUDICA AWOKE THE NEXT MORNING, SHE heard the rumble of horses approaching the camp. She sat up, alarm flowing through her. The camp was just waking up, and she saw others turn toward the sound of approaching horses, unease flickering across their faces.

She lurched to her feet, pulling her cloak around her and turning toward a hovering guard.

"Stay by my daughters," she ordered, jerking her head toward her still sleeping daughters, who slept next to Kensa on their animal pelts.

She moved to the edge of the camp where Mael, Judoc, Cadell, and several other warriors stood, surveying the approaching men. Her tension dissipated when she saw that the approaching men were natives, wearing dark-belted tunics rather than the crimson tunics and armor of the Romans. There were roughly one hundred of them.

Once they drew close, the three men who rode at the head dismounted from their horses.

One man, tall and broad-shouldered, with dark hair and the long mustache of a chieftain, stepped forward.

"We seek the chieftain of the Iceni."

"I'm the chieftain," Boudica said, squaring her shoulders and holding her head high.

"We received your message about joining the rebellion . . . and heard what you've done to that stain of a Roman capital on our lands." His eyes swept past her to the burning ashes of Camulodunum. "We had to see for ourselves . . . and join the fight."

The man was Yannik, chieftain of the Cantiaci tribe. He told her the rest of their men were camped out to the south; they numbered in the thousands. Yannik and the other two chieftains of the Durotriges and Belgae tribes, Corentin and Gael, both as muscular and broad as Yannik, had come to a truce of peace between their previously warring tribes.

"We have a larger enemy now," Yannik said with a scowl. "One who has dwelled on our lands for too long. We tried to rise against them once, but they overwhelmed us. There has been a tentative peace, but they tax us to occupy our lands, and send our men to die in their legions. It must end."

"It will," Boudica said, a surge of determination coursing through her. "With our tribes working together, we can purge them from our lands."

"Where do you march next?" asked Corentin.

"Londinium. It's a small Roman trading post; there's nothing but a small fort there for protection. Catus Decianus and his men are stationed there." Rage swelled within her at the thought of Catus. "I only ask that when the time comes . . . you leave Catus and his men to me."

She'd feared the men would protest, but they nodded their agreement. Word had spread about what had happened to her and her daughters.

When the chieftains returned with their men, Boudica was eating her morning meal with her daughters; bread and ale from the provisions they'd brought with them. As she ate, her gaze swept over the mingling tribes. The men regarded each other with wary caution; over the years they had all been enemies at some point, going to battle with each other over the lands the Romans had taken for themselves. She could detect hints of tension in the looks of distrust shared between the warriors of the tribes as they separated into their own areas of the camp. Once again, she prayed they could set aside their age-old rivalries to focus on their common enemy.

Kensa, sensing Boudica's distraction, took her daughters away to wash in the nearby river.

Boudica stood as they left, her eyes still surveying the tense warriors of the tribes with unease. Cadell approached, and she stiffened at the harsh look on his face.

"The chieftains have agreed to work together," she said, her body stiffening with defense. "There shouldn't be any—"

"That's not what I'm here about," Cadell interjected. "I want to know what you plan to do after we reach Londinium and you kill Catus and his men."

Boudica studied him with a frown. His expression was tight, his mouth pressed into a thin line.

"I'll keep fighting," Boudica said, surprised at his question. She pulled herself to her full height, glaring at him. "Till the Romans are gone from these lands, or the breath's gone from my body. If you still doubt me—"

"I do not doubt you," he said. "But the cycle of

revenge is never-ending. I saw your face when you asked the other chieftains to leave the killing of Catus and his men to you. After you kill Catus and his men —if you even get to them—"

"I will," Boudica hissed, clenching her fists at her sides.

"This rebellion needs to be about more than revenge."

"Tell me—what is it you fight for?" Boudica bit out. How dare Cadell question her motives? He knew what had happened to her family and her reasons for wanting to fight.

"My tribe," Cadell replied without hesitation. "My wife died while birthing our first child years ago. Since that day, I've vowed that my only purpose would be to serve my tribe. Nothing else matters to me."

His voice was firm and unwavering, but Boudica saw the shadow of grief in his eyes.

"We all have our motives," Boudica said, her tone softening. "The end result is the same."

"Boudica."

She turned to face Mael as he approached, grateful for the interruption. Mael's face was taut with worry.

"What is it?"

"A lone rider has approached the camp. He claims to be a messenger of the Brigantes queen, Cartimandua."

Hope replaced her remnant anger, and she

exchanged a glance with Cadell, who looked startled. The Brigantes hadn't responded to her message; she'd assumed they refused to join the fight. But if they were joining them . . . a powerful northern tribe added to their ranks could change everything.

"She wishes to meet with you," Mael continued. "Alone."

19

Isle of Mona

The dead bodies of the druids littered the rocky banks of Mona, like discarded garbage Suetonius had seen strewn about the outskirts of Rome. He watched as soldiers dragged the bodies from the shore, depositing them into swampy mass graves.

He sat with Tertius and the other soldiers on the adjoining beach, eating charred meat and bread, along with ale from their stores. Suetonius was the only one who paid attention to the bodies. He finally tore his eyes away, taking a swig of ale. The battle had been fierce but quick; his trained soldiers easily slaying the druids with their superior fighting skills. When there were only a few druids left, they'd shouted prayers to their gods in their native tongue, before slitting their own throats.

"Filthy barbarians," Tertius had seethed, spitting on their bodies.

Suetonius had felt no triumph, no sense of accomplishment after the battle—the massacre. Instead, he felt oddly hollow. He'd slaughtered countless barbarians on behalf of the empire, ruthlessly cutting down men and women, the young and the old —anyone who defied the might of Rome. He'd become good at it, with two emperors promoting him through the ranks; it was why Nero had sent him to Britannia.

He took another swig of ale, willing the hollowness to subside. He wasn't much of a drinker; he preferred his mind clear, but he'd been drinking much more as of late.Shortly after the massacre he'd had several cups of ale.

"I was governor of the Mauretania province . . . before I was sent here."

He didn't realize he'd spoken aloud until the men around him fell respectfully silent. He continued, absently, "The locals often rebelled against us. After the last rebellion . . . we rounded up the villagers to watch as we executed the leaders. There was this woman. . . her sons had just been killed. She looked at me and said, 'If men like the Romans can rule the world . . . our gods have abandoned us.' And then— just like those druids—she slit her own throat. Just so."

He mimed the gesture, drawing his finger across the line of his throat, lost in the dark memory. His soldiers were silent, and he could sense their discomfort. Tertius was the only one brave enough to speak up.

"They fight us because they know no better."

Paulinus let out a short laugh, giving him a twisted smile. He raised his cup to his lips and took another swig.

"I once thought like you."

He closed his eyes, now realizing how much that woman's words affected him, years after she'd spoken them. At first, he'd dismissed her words as the ravings of a savage. But after several more violent campaigns, with the weeping of women and the howl of dying men filling his ears, barbarian blood staining his fine cloak and tunic, her words kept returning, reverberating in his mind.

"Governor Paulinus!"

Suetonius's eyes flew open as a Roman messenger approached, his tunic damp and stained with mud as he dismounted from his horse.

He frowned. The trek north to Mona was a difficult one. For the messenger to have traveled all this way—

Suetonius shot to his feet, his reverie and self-reflection dissipating, and he was once again the trained, dutiful Roman soldier.

"What is it?" he demanded, as the messenger drew near.

"There's been an uprising by a barbarian army,"

the messenger replied, out of breath. "They've destroyed our capital."

Suetonius's horse galloped through the countryside. The sunrise had just begun its ascent, illuminating its lush greenery. It would have been too cumbersome of a task to get the large contingent of men he'd taken with him from Mona to Londinium by the next day, so he'd only taken a small cavalry of fifty soldiers with him. He'd left almost immediately, the effect of drink dissipating as he'd ridden. He'd traveled all night, only taking brief stops for his soldiers to relieve themselves and allow their horses to rest. The razor-sharp focus he'd honed during all his years as a soldier and then a general had been his savior; there was no panic as he rode, even as he recalled the facts the messenger had relayed.

A barbarian army, led by a woman, numbering in the tens of thousands. Camulodunum burned to the ground, its citizens slaughtered. Another legion of Roman soldiers, sent to rescue the colonia, slaughtered by a smaller barbarian army. The barbarian army now moving south toward Londinium.

There had been uprisings before in Britannia, but they had all been swiftly and brutally put down. But this one was different—more foreboding. The warring tribes of Britannia were working together as one, a woman at their head, and they'd destroyed the

Roman capital, a symbol of Roman dominance over Britannia.

Suetonius kicked the sides of his horse for speed when he saw the outline of Londinium in the distance. He'd only traveled to Londinium once and disliked it. It was too small of a trading post to bring in much coin to Rome, and he didn't like sparing the soldiers who guarded it from its miniscule fort, especially when he learned the soldiers spent most of their time drinking and whoring rather than patrolling. But Catus insisted it would become a valuable trading post for the empire and preferred to reside there rather than in Camulodunum. That may have saved his life. The barbarians would have torn him apart had he been in the capital.

He and his men rode into Londinium, which was comprised of a cluster of buildings made of wood, clay, and timber. The only defense, he noted with a sliver of unease, was a small fort on a nearby hill.

As he approached the fort where Catus was stationed, a sudden anger seized him. The messenger hadn't provided a specific cause for the uprising by previously docile tribes, but Suetonius suspected that Catus had something to do with it. He recalled his last discussion with Catus back at his residence in Camulodunum. *I will not negotiate with the barbarians.*

"Governor," Catus said with a forced smile, stepping out from the fort's entrance as Suetonius dismounted. Quintus, the general whose legion was slaughtered by the barbarians, trailed him out. They both gave Suetonius respectful nods. "I thought you were tending to the barbarian priests in Mona."

Suetonius said nothing, stalking toward Catus with quiet rage. Catus took a faltering step back. For once, he wasn't looking at him with imperiousness. He was afraid of him. Good.

"Our capital city's been destroyed and one of our best legions slaughtered," Suetonius hissed. "Surely you received notice from our scouts of a large army approaching. Why was I not notified until now?"

"We weren't expecting those numbers," Catus said stiffly. "I was told that it was a small army of women. I did not think—"

"The Iceni and Trinovantes have been our allies," Suetonius interrupted, narrowing his eyes. "What caused this?"

Catus hesitated, a look of guilt flickering across his expression.

"What. Caused. This?" Suetonius repeated.

"The client king of the Iceni died. I called in our rights to their lands and property; their queen disobeyed my orders. As punishment, I had her flogged and her daughters . . . her daughters were left to the attentions of my men."

Suetonius stilled. He was ashamed to realize there was a time when such actions would not have affected him. But now, fury and revulsion roiled through him.

"Prasutagus was the wealthiest of the native

chiefs," Suetonius forced himself to say, between clenched teeth. "How convenient that he should suddenly die without a male heir. What was his cause of death?"

Catus went pale, averting his gaze.

"A sudden illness, Governor," he answered. "It was most unfortunate. I don't like your implications. I had nothing to do with—"

"What are their numbers?" Suetonius interrupted, waving away Catus's words. He had no time for the snake's lies.

"Twenty or thirty thousand." Quintus was the one who spoke up, stepping forward.

Something foreign roiled through Suetonius—something foreign to him. Panic. The uprisings he'd put down before had been smaller and much easier to contain.

He turned, studying the scant number of Roman soldiers who stood at attention. He then turned to face Londinium, now just waking up. A solution settled in on him, one he was reluctant to admit out loud. But he had no choice. They were gravely outnumbered.

"We cannot stand against them."

Catus looked at him with disbelief while outrage filled Quintus's eyes.

"That barbarian bitch and her army wiped out my legion. I refuse to allow—" Quintus began.

"For this battle," Suetonius amended. "We don't have the numbers . . .we'd be slaughtered where we stand. My other men are still in Mona, other legions are scattered around the province. Even if my other soldiers could make it here in time from Mona, we'd still be greatly outnumbered. If we—as the remaining Roman defenses—are decimated, all of Britannia will fall. Londinium must be sacrificed; we can rebuild."

Though Catus and Quintus looked mutinous, they didn't protest further.

"Your men are coming with me to regroup with my soldiers," Suetonius said to Catus. "As for the citizens, advise them to evacuate. But first . . . who are the soldiers who violated the Icenian queen's daughters?"

Catus paled, and for a moment Suetonius thought he wouldn't reply. Finally, he turned and signaled to three soldiers, who stepped forward. Their expressions were stoic, but he could see traces of fear in their eyes. Suetonius surveyed them for a long moment before speaking.

"Catus, you and these men are to remain here. I'm leaving behind a small detachment of soldiers to assist the civilians as they depart. And to ensure that you do not leave."

He stepped back, signaling to a dozen of his own soldiers, a dark satisfaction filling him as blood drained from Catus's face.

"Ensure that Catus and his men are bound and placed into their barracks," he told Tertius, who nodded.

"Governor, I must protest. As procurator, I have the right—" Catus sputtered.

"As procurator, you have incited a rebellion and your response was insufficient. You will face the consequences of your actions."

He gave Catus a fierce glare before turning to Quintus and pulling him aside.

"I'll send an urgent message to Rome requesting more legions. But for now, I need you to ride out to surrounding forts to secure more soldiers."

"I will send one of my men to secure the soldiers —if you will allow it, Governor. The barbarian queen slaughtered my men; I must face her."

Suetonius regarded him warily; he didn't want one of his top generals slaughtered by the barbarians. But by the fierce look on Quintus's face, he suspected he would remain here no matter what Suetonius ordered.

"Very well," Suetonius said finally. "I must ask . . . did you make contact with the barbarian queen during the attack?"

"Yes," Quintus said, his eyes going dark. "She said . . . she said that if Rome does not leave these lands, she will kill every man, woman and child who stands in her way."

A chill crept through Suetonius; he recalled the hatred lurking in Boudica's eyes at the last diplomatic feast he'd attended at her home, the simmering fury she couldn't hide.

He had no doubt she would carry out her threat.

20

Boudica's heart pounded with anticipation as she rode with Judoc and two other guards north, trailing Cartimandua's messenger, Loic. Both Mael and Cadell had cautioned her against meeting with Cartimandua, reminding her of how she'd betrayed another native who'd opposed the Romans years before. But Boudica thought it was worth the risk and prayed she could convince her to join their army.

Loic led them to the lands just north of Camulodunum, where the Trinovantes lands met the lands of another tribe, the Coritani. Loic told her Cartimandua had ridden south to meet with the Coritani after a dispute between their tribes, just as news of the rebellion spread—and when she'd learned of Boudica's message.

Cartimandua was waiting for Boudica in a thatch-roofed home on the outskirts of the Coritani lands. Loic gestured for Boudica and her guards to enter, and she saw a petite woman standing before the burning hearth. She turned, surveying Boudica with impudent, gray eyes. Her long, blond hair was braided and wound on the back of her head in a coiled bun. She wore a tunic made of fine green silk with a golden torc adorning her arm and neck, and golden earrings with carnelian stones dangling from her ears. She'd seen the same type of stone on finger rings the Roman officials wore, and wondered darkly if they were a gift from her rumored lover, the Roman governor, Suetonius Paulinus.

Though she was small in stature, and Boudica towered over her, Cartimandua had a regal air to her. This was a woman used to command. Cartimandua smiled at Boudica, though there was no warmth in her eyes. She turned to Boudica's guards, who flanked her.

"My guards are outside. Your queen and I can speak alone."

Judoc stiffened, but Boudica gave him a reassuring nod, gesturing for him and the guards to leave.

When they were alone, Cartimandua's smile faded, and she stepped forward with narrowed eyes.

"You are a bold one. To rise against Rome, your tribe's allies. I thought the Iceni were a loyal tribe."

"It's the Romans who betrayed us," Boudica said, bristling at the reprimand in her tone. "And we were never their allies; we didn't have a choice."

"You are not the first to rise against Rome," Cartimandua murmured, shaking her head. "I assume you've heard the tragic tale of Caratacus, the rebel who came to me for help."

"Yes. You turned him over to Rome in chains," Boudica said, her chest tightening.

"Why should I treat you any different?"

"Because I'm a fellow native queen of these lands," Boudica returned. "I think you allied with Rome because you felt you had no choice, and you did what was necessary to keep your people safe and alive. My husband did the same, as did my father. But the Romans betrayed them both. Yesterday, my army destroyed the Roman capital, and we killed many of their soldiers. Other tribes have joined us and our numbers have grown. Victory over Rome is possible."

"The Romans have been kind to me and my people," Cartimandua said, her mouth pressed into a thin line. "If I were to join you, many of my people will die."

"If you do nothing, many of your people may still die," Boudica said firmly. She stepped forward, grateful for her towering height; it gave her a commanding presence that clashed with Cartimandua's imperious one.

"The Iceni were loyal to the Romans and did what they asked. We only asked them to uphold my husband's will. Do you—do you know what they did to my daughters?" she asked, unable to stop her voice from wavering.

Cartimandua's eyes filled with a brief sliver of

pity before it was gone, and her eyes went cold once more.

"It was tragic what happened to your daughters. But the procurator's actions are not the fault of Rome as a whole. And . . . I heard it was your foolish defiance which caused Catus to react so violently."

Boudica tensed, struggling to maintain her calm. Mael had been right to caution her against coming to Cartimandua.

"You are a fool to assume you can remove the Romans from these lands," Cartimandua continued, her eyes flashing. "They have conquered most of the known world. Those who defy them end up slaughtered or slaves. I made a choice long ago, that my people would thrive, even under their rule. You and the other native tribes may think me a traitor, but I have saved my people. And I will continue to do so."

Boudica gave Cartimandua a smile of her own, one that displayed no humor, no kindness. Cartimandua tensed at the look in her eyes, as Boudica took another threatening step forward.

"You are acting out of cowardice and nothing more. I would rather fight and die than live as a Roman slave. When your people start to hate you for bowing down to the Romans, or when the Romans inevitably betray you, I hope you remember every detail of this moment, as I remember every detail of the day my husband was murdered and my daughters raped by the men you call allies."

She spat the last word, her fury spiking. She

forced herself to stalk out, leaving a pale and shaken Cartimandua in her wake.

Later, Boudica and her army rode away from the incinerated remains of Camulodunum as the sun rose high in the sky, making their way south to Londinium. She rode at the head of the combined armies with Cadell and the other chieftains. Their combined army had swelled to the tens of thousands, the warriors marching in the front with their families trailing behind them at the rear, moving over the countryside in a great swarm.

"I will kill a thousand Romans today," Yannik boasted. "Rip their heads off with my bare hands and mount them to my horses."

"I will tear off their armor and bleed them out with my dagger until they scream," Corentin growled. "They call us savage barbarians. I will show them how savage I can be."

"I will make them feast on their own insides," Gael said with a grin. "And then I will tear their limbs off with my blade while they still breathe."

The chieftains continued their boasting, but Boudica did not take part. Cartimandua's words continued to fill her mind. *You are a fool to assume you can remove the Romans from these lands*

She forced the traitor queen's words from her mind, focusing on what lay ahead: Londinium. Catus and his soldiers. Her revenge. She would take her time with him; he didn't deserve a quick death.

The thought of her looming revenge invigorated her, and she kicked the sides of her horse to quicken its pace.

They'd been riding for some time when Boudica spotted the burnt-out hollow of a village to the east. She frowned, unease coiling around her.

"Keep the army marching," she told the other chieftains. "I'll rejoin you."

She turned her horse to gallop toward the burned village, trailed by Judoc, Cadell, Mael and several of her guards. A chill like the winter's frost filled Boudica as they drew near. She could already see the remnant traces of fire—hollowed-out buildings, ash littering the ground. Fury gripped her as she took it in. *The Romans*.

Boudica dismounted, looking around. The village could have been a replica of her own. There were the familiar thatch-roofed roundhouses and farmsteads, still standing upright despite the fire. A large meeting and dining hall was situated near the village square, and the prominent roundhouse at the rear of the village must have one been a chieftain's home.

She could imagine the square filled with revelers during one of the harvest festivals, the roar of combat challenges from the chieftain's home, the villagers following druid priests out to the surrounding forests to witness and partake in their rituals.

But now the village lay still and empty, a corpse

devoid of life. Why had the Romans burned the village? Had they killed all of its citizens as well? Raped the women? Carted them off to be slaves?

"This wasn't the Romans," Mael said, his voice low at her side. "Your father and I used to see many like this during the early years of the Roman invasion."

He gestured to a pit on the northern side of the village. Boudica hadn't noticed it before, and her stomach tightened.

She approached it, and froze. Inside lay a multitude of dead bodies: men, women, and children. Many of them were emaciated, their throats slit.

She pressed her hand to her mouth. She knew of human sacrifices, Rozen had told her it was common when she herself was a girl, but practiced less now. But even then, it was only a lone volunteer, sacrificed willingly to appease the gods. Rozen had told her many natives had taken to human sacrifice after the Romans came, to appease the gods and expel the Romans from their lands. But to commit a mass sacrifice such as this one, the villagers must have been truly desperate.

"They did this to themselves," she whispered.

Behind her, Cadell and Judoc remained silent, but their expressions were turbulent. Mael sank to his knees before the pit. He held out his hands and closed his eyes, whispering a prayer.

"Their sacrifice was a plea for mercy to the gods," Cadell murmured, moving forward to stand at her side. His blue eyes were distant as he continued, "I was a boy when the Romans first came. The crops had failed; many in our village were starving. We'd lost many men during the fighting. I only lived because my father was chieftain. He didn't want to surrender to the Romans. They sent me away to live with my uncle. I can still see my mother's eyes . . . I knew what they were going to do, what they all were going to do. But I was still horrified when I returned to find they'd all sacrificed themselves. Just like these villagers."

A rush of empathy surged through Boudica as she took in the raw grief in his eyes. For all his outward gruffness, Cadell was someone who'd suffered great loss: his parents, then his wife and child, and had buried his pain, choosing only to focus on leading his tribe.

She saw Judoc's usually hard eyes soften as he glanced at Cadell. After their initial tension, Judoc and Cadell had argued less, and now the men treated each other with grudging respect.

She looked down at the bodies as Mael continued to pray. Even if it was self-sacrifice, the Romans were responsible for this. The Romans had caused too many to suffer.

"I don't deny I fight for revenge, Cadell," she whispered. "But I also fight for my people . . . for all the natives of these lands. These people didn't deserve to die like this. Nor did yours. The Romans must suffer for what they've done."

When her army descended upon Londinium, Boudica's fury had swelled, the memory of the dead villagers fresh in her mind.

Londinium was mostly abandoned when her army descended upon it like a searing fire, but they took out their fury on the buildings and the small contingent of Roman soldiers who tried to defend it, like wolves devouring helpless prey.

But Boudica only wanted one Roman. Among the chaos of fighting around her, she approached a dying Roman soldier. A spear was wedged into his chest, his eyes wild with pain.

She knelt down, pressing the blade of her sword to his throat. He cried out in agony as she pressed it down, and his blood spilled like a crimson river onto his tunic. She leaned down, so he could hear her among the grunts of the warriors and the raging fires around them.

"Catus Decianus. Where is he?"

The soldier opened his mouth, but he was too weak to speak. Instead, his eyes strayed toward the east. She followed his gaze to a fort on the outskirts of Londinium.

Boudica straightened and darted to her horse. She mounted it and galloped to the fort, her pulse racing. This building wasn't as heavily fortified as the ones Mael had described to her—there was no high brick wall guarding it, and it was made of wood—easy to burn.

As soon as she arrived, several soldiers emerged from the fort and charged toward her. She leapt from her horse, taking out her sword as they surrounded her. But two soldiers were shot down with arrows before she could strike. She whirled as Judoc rode up behind her, his weapon at the ready.

Another soldier charged toward her with an enraged snarl; she recognized him as Quintus, the Roman general she'd set free with a warning during their ambush outside of Camulodunum. He took her by surprise, kicking her back to the ground, his eyes filled with fury.

Boudica was reminded of her father's foot on her throat during that combat challenge years ago, and for just a moment panic flared within her, as Quintus placed his sandaled foot onto her throat and pressed down, robbing her of air.

"Barbarian whore!" he seethed.

But Boudica was no longer a naïve girl of seventeen. She twisted out of the way as he thrust his sword down. She reached for her sword, leaping to her feet and stabbing him straight through his neck, watching with dark pleasure as he sank to his knees before slumping forward, dead.

Next to her, Judoc dispatched the other two soldiers. Still speckled with Quintus's blood, Boudica charged into the fort, ignoring his warning shouts.

But inside, there were no soldiers waiting to

attack. Instead, she found a row of barracks, wooden slabs hammered over their doorways.

Frowning, she moved over to one, using the hilt of her sword to crack it open. Disbelief filled her when it revealed a tied-up Roman soldier, glaring at her.

She stilled. This was one of the soldiers who'd gone to Kensa's home to attack her daughters; she recalled the jagged scar that ran down his jaw. Heart hammering, she exchanged a puzzled look with Judoc, and together they removed the wooden slabs of the other barracks, revealing several other tied-up soldiers—all soldiers who'd participated in the assault of her daughters.

But it was the last room that held the greatest prize of all. Catus sat huddled inside, his hands and feet bound. He froze at the sight of her, his eyes filling with both hatred and fear.

"Why are they imprisoned like this?" Judoc asked, suspicion lacing his tone.

Boudica studied Catus, a dark giddiness sweeping over her. She didn't know why the soldiers were held like this; perhaps it was simply the will of the gods to allow her her justice. She whispered a prayer of thanks to Garmangabis before stepping into Catus's quarters.

His eyes widened with panic as he met the wildness of her gaze. She imagined she must look frightening; still splattered with Quintus's blood, her face covered entirely by green war paint.

As she stepped closer, Catus's fear seemed to

take hold, and he scooted back as far into the room as his bonds would allow. Cadell was right about him. He was a coward; nothing without his soldiers to do his bidding.

She knelt down before him, stripping him of his cloak, and then using her sword to rip open his tunic until he was nude, just as he'd done to her. His eyes widened, panic contorting his features.

Boudica dropped her sword, reaching for a dagger she had tucked away beneath her tunic. She stepped forward, her voice dropping to a whisper, echoing what he'd said to her on that fateful day.

"I will take great pleasure in this."

She turned to Judoc.

"Keep your eyes on the other soldiers; they're next. If any of our men come, send them away. This will take time."

Judoc obliged, leaving her alone with Catus. She turned back to face Catus, closing her eyes.

When she opened them again, she allowed her maelstrom of rage to take over.

21

Roman Fort Kiluronus
Northwest of Verulamium

Suetonius stood outside the Roman fort of Kiluronus, next to Tertius, watching as soldiers filed in. They came from various posts around Britannia, soldiers from several legions and other local auxiliaries.

A young general by the name of Aelius stood before him. Aelius was one of the few soldiers who'd survived the barbarian attack on Camulodunum, riding to Kiluronus under the cover of night until he'd arrived. He'd told Suetonius what he'd witnessed at Camulodunum: the size of the barbarian army, their fury, and their leadership by a queen named Boudica.

Aelius was performing a manual count of the soldiers, but Suetonius didn't need a count to know their numbers were meager—thousands compared to the barbarian army which now numbered in the tens of thousands. His scout had estimated nearly eighty thousand strong. He'd sent a messenger to Rome requesting more legions, but with the speed of the barbarian army, he suspected that by the time the messenger arrived in Rome, it would be too late.

"I count eight thousand," Aelius said as the last soldier filed in.

Suetonius pressed his fingers to his temples. A steady throbbing there had plagued him since he rode away from Londinium, leaving Catus and his men to their deaths.

"The scouts think the barbarians will march to Verulamium next. It's right in their path; and it's our largest remaining settlement," Tertius said grimly.

Suetonius didn't respond. For the first time in his military career, his men were losing to a barbarian army. He wondered if word had already reached Rome, if the emperor knew that his uncle's prized province was on the verge of being lost.

"We can't let them destroy any more of our settlements," Tertius continued. "I can lead a detachment of soldiers to Verulamium to hold them off."

"No," Suetonius said curtly. "Send an evacuation order to all who can to leave the settlement. I cannot spare the men."

"If it's just a small detachment—"

"You know the numbers of the barbarian army. I will not sacrifice my remaining soldiers to fight a battle they will not win."

"We're not even attempting to hold off the barbarians," Tertius said, his face going rigid with anger. "You let them have Londinium. Catus let them have Camulodunum."

"You seem to forget that I am your superior, Tertius," Suetonius said, turning to glower at Tertius. The throbbing in his temples increased, and he clenched his teeth.

"I don't believe another colonia needs to be sacrificed," Tertius continued, recklessly.

Suetonius had never struck a soldier, had never lost his temper when one defied his orders. A simmering anger had seized him, and he had to force himself to hold still, to regulate his breathing. He was on the verge of losing Britannia; he had no time to deal with this simpering upstart.

"I've been putting down uprisings since before you stepped foot onto a battlefield, *soldier*, and I've learned that small battles mean nothing. This province will fall altogether if my remaining men die defending settlements that can easily be rebuilt. I will not have my orders challenged."

Tertius fell silent, but his expression was mutinous.

"I'm going to join the soldiers already at Verulamium. I'll stand with them against the barbarians," Tertius said. His voice was calmer now, but still laced with anger.

"Do you want me to seize him, Governor?"

Aelius asked, as Tertius stalked away before Suetonius could reply.

"No," Suetonius said shortly. "If he chooses to die . . . it's his death. Let him go."

SUETONIUS TRIED TO CONCENTRATE AS HE discussed plans for the offensive against the barbarian army with Aelius and two other generals, but it was difficult to pull himself from the thoughts of self-reprimand that swirled through his mind. He kept recalling the malaise that plagued him before and after the massacre in Mona; the hollowness. Perhaps it was this wavering that made him neglectful of his duties, and he'd not given his proper attentions to the native tribes. He should have visited the tribes more often for matters of diplomacy rather than allowing the greedy Catus to handle such concerns. Perhaps then he would have sensed the tribes' discontentment and handled it before it grew into the fiery rebellion that now swept over Britannia.

"Governor."

He looked up as a young messenger entered the room. Suetonius stilled, bracing himself for more bad news.

"Queen Cartimandua of the Brigantes tribe is here."

Relief filled him. He found Cartimandua in his private quarters: petite, regal and lovely, surveying him with shrewd eyes as he entered. He admired Cartimandua, and not just for her willing alliance with Rome, but for her sharp mind, her shrewd intelligence that he'd never encountered before in a woman. He didn't need to ask her why she was here; she had to know of the uprising and the massive barbarian army laying waste to the lands.

"I've met her," Cartimandua said, by way of greeting. "The queen who leads this rebellion. She's fierce. Tall as a man," Cartimandua continued, and he thought he saw a glint of reluctant admiration in her eyes. "I can see why men follow her."

"Do you follow her?" he asked sharply.

Was that why she was here? Was there an army with her, waiting to take out the Roman fort?

Cartimandua laughed, looking genuinely amused.

"I wouldn't be here if that were so. I think Queen Boudica is very brave, but a fool, and I told her so. My spies tell me she intends to march on Verulamium."

"We're aware," he said with a scowl. "Is there anything else you know? Anything that can help?"

"I think that she can be reasoned with," Cartimandua said, after a brief pause.

Suetonius barked out an unamused laugh.

"I disagree. She slaughtered innocent Roman citizens in a temple in Camulodunum. That is not someone who can be reasoned with. I will not make peace with the woman who rebels against us."

"That isn't what I'm suggesting. But perhaps

some agreement can be reached to prevent more bloodshed."

"We may be allies, but I do not take orders from you," he returned. He straightened, studying her with sudden suspicion. "Why did you not capture her when you met her? If you were truly Rome's ally—"

"She came with her guards, and I would have suffered the wrath of her massive army had I tried to take her," Cartimandua interrupted. "And my suggestion is just that—a suggestion, not an order. At the heart of all this, Boudica is a grief-stricken widow, an anguished mother. I heard you left her Catus and his men to kill. If you tell her that was your doing, perhaps she can tame her army. Perhaps all they want is for you to cede to their demands."

"They want us gone from their lands," Suetonius gritted out. "That will never happen."

"I know. But what if compromise is possible?"

"It isn't," he said shortly. He crossed to a table at the far side of the room, pouring himself a cup of ale. The pounding in his temple had begun again, and he closed his eyes.

A sweet, honeyed scent infused his nostrils, and he felt a soft hand run up his arm. He turned; Cartimandua now stood close at his side.

"That is all I came here to tell you. But . . . is there anything else I can do?" Cartimandua's voice was a seductive whisper in his ear. "Any other comfort I can offer?"

He met her gray eyes, recalling the night they'd

shared after a diplomatic meeting the year prior: her soft curves against his, his lips against her skin. She'd offered him one of her attendants, but the young woman had been quaking and pale, unable to look him in the eye. Cartimandua had dismissed her before stepping forward to press her lips against his.

It had been some time since he'd had a woman, and her offer was tempting. But he stepped away from her.

"No," he said, his tone hard. "You should return to Brigantia. Allies of Rome, even native ones, are not safe until we put down the rebellion."

Cartimandua drew back, not looking even slightly disappointed. It was another thing he admired about her; her utter lack of sentiment. She gave him a nod of farewell before leaving his quarters.

He quelled the sliver of regret that filled him at her departure. His odd prevarication as of late had weakened him; he'd allowed that barbarian woman's words from all those years ago to affect him. He couldn't allow another woman to make him lose focus. He would defeat this barbarian queen, Boudica, and slaughter her on the battlefield.

22

The brooch Antedios had given her years ago glistened in the firelight. Boudica reached out to wipe away the speckle of blood that marred its surface, rolling it around in her hands.

The army had set up camp on the outskirts of the scorched Londinium. The warriors were confident after yet another victory, and their shouts and cries as they boasted, feasted, and drank, punctuated the night air.

From where Boudica sat by her personal bonfire, she could see Kensa standing watch over her daughters with Elouan at her side. His hand was entwined in hers, and Kensa's face was flushed with happiness as he bent down to place a kiss on her cheek.

Nolwenn sat next to them with a senior bard of the tribe, listening intently as he spoke to her.

Brighid hovered next to a group of children, who

were chasing each other or engaging in mock sword fights with sticks. She bent down to pick up a stick, approaching two boys in the midst of a mock fight. They regarded her for a moment before stepping aside to let her join in. As she fought with the boys, a shadow of a smile appeared on Brighid's face, and relief swept through Boudica. Her daughters—and Kensa—were slowly coming back to life.

Boudica returned her focus to the brooch in her hands. She'd spent a long time with Catus and each of his soldiers, reveling in the darkness that swelled within her as she used her dagger to tear at their flesh, taking pleasure in their cries for mercy. The darkness had become a living thing, whispering in her ear to draw out their pain for as long as possible, and she had, until their blood had splattered her own skin, mingling with her sweat, and their whimpers had turned into long, guttural death rattles. The dark voice had continued to whisper in her ear, even after Catus and his soldiers were dead.

You should have listened to me all along. You were never meant to be a wife, daughter and mother. This is what you are. Had you listened to me, your husband would be alive, your daughters still innocent.

"You've not said a word since the battle."

The dark whispers ceased, and Boudica looked up as Mael approached, taking a seat on the ground opposite her.

"I dreamed of what I'd say to Catus and his men if I ever got to take my revenge," she whispered. "I dreamed of how it would feel to tear their flesh with my sword, the sound of their cries as they begged for mercy, the rattle in their throats as they drew their last breath."

Mael studied her, his dark eyes knowing. "You liked it. You fear you liked it too much."

She met his eyes, startled. Were her feelings that plain?

"Yes," she admitted. "I keep seeking the grief that's been there since Prasutagus died, since my daughters were attacked. But all I feel now . . . is rage. And it hasn't lessened, not even with Catus's death."

"Then you must use it."

"The rage? The darkness? I don't want—"

"It's always been in you. It's been in many of us since the Romans came and subdued us. Some can push it aside, others cannot. You are one of those who must use your rage. Don't feel ashamed of the darkness that helps you do what you must. It's what will lead our people to victory. Look at them," he said, gesturing to the vast army that surrounded them. "There is still much to be done. These people crave liberation from Rome. You are leading them toward it."

She thought of their lands free of Roman control. She thought of working in unity with other tribes, of living in peace.

But would she ever be able to return to a life of normalcy again? Or would this darkness always persist, always linger? She thought of Catus's eyes, his face covered with blood, as he begged her to *please stop please for the love of all the gods stop*. But she hadn't stopped.

How could she be a loving mother to her girls with this darkness raging inside her?

She closed her eyes, rubbing her temples. How foolish she'd been as a young girl, dreaming of becoming a warrior. She'd imagined it as nothing but honor, glory and victory. Instead, it was darkness, rage, blood, death.

"What did you see, Mael?" she asked suddenly, opening her eyes as a memory seized her. "During the first rebellion, when my father died . . . I asked you to perform a divination. You said you saw my face."

"I saw exactly what I told you. Blood. Fire. Your face. I didn't know you'd lead a rebellion . . . I just sensed something momentous was to come, and it would be because of you."

"The night Prasutagus died . . . I had a strange dream. I saw myself standing on a field filled with blood and edged by fire."

Mael didn't look surprised by this. "The gods may have been showing you what was to come."

Boudica suppressed a wave of frustration. The dream had shown her nothing; it just filled her with foreboding.

"Can you perform another divination? To see how this will all end?"

He gave her a sad smile. "I've tried, but the gods

have shown me nothing. We make our own end, Boudica. But our army has destroyed two Roman settlements. For now, we have the Romans on the run. In these lands, there hasn't been an uprising of this size before, not since the time of the first Caesar. I pray victory is near. But we must keep moving forward."

He left her alone, and Boudica allowed his words to soothe her as she stood to approach her daughters and Kensa.

As she walked through the camp, she surveyed the mass of warriors and their families. There was a hum of giddiness and excitement among the large army; laughter and the buzz of conversation filled the air.

A routine of sorts had developed after each battle. The warriors would share the loot they'd taken from the destroyed Roman settlement and share it with their families and tribesmen, adding Roman wines and stores of meat and bread to the meager provisions they'd brought with them, enjoying the food during celebratory feasts.

The chieftains would hold court over the combat challenges and celebratory feasts, shouting encouragements and gifting the winners with loot and promises of land when they returned home. Boudica had even seen Gael and Yannik join several combat challenges themselves.

The bards would gather at the edge of the camp, verbally composing their tale of the rebellion, often joined by the druid priests who were expected to know every detail of the tale for future generations of priests. Boudica would often see Nolwenn huddled with the bards, who'd taken a liking to her—and not just because she was the daughter of the chief rebel. Mael told her Nolwenn had a gift for telling tales.

Brighid would spar with the boys of the tribe, sons of warriors, all of whom looked surprised by her natural fighting abilities.

Kensa and Elouan would walk hand in hand on the outskirts of camp, their heads bowed low, sometimes sharing a kiss when they thought no one was watching.

She'd noticed that Cadell and Judoc had become increasingly friendly; they fought each other in good-natured combat challenges. Judoc had gruffly told her he respected Cadell as a warrior.

When Mael wasn't advising her or the other chieftains, he spent much of his time with the other priests, praying for the fallen—the Romans and the natives—and for the continued victory of the native tribes.

Boudica walked past a group of warriors, who stood with Gael, and their words pulled her back to the present. She froze.

"When we get to Verulamium, I'll drag the natives out of their homes and strangle them with my bare hands," one man growled.

"We should take their heads and leave them out for their Roman lovers to find," another man spat.

"No, we should burn the natives in the Roman homes they've built for themselves," Gael said, and the men grumbled their agreement.

Boudica halted in her tracks. The army was marching to Verulamium next, the nearest Roman settlement. Mael had told her it was populated by the Catuvellauni, a native tribe who was loyal to Rome. But Boudica had no intention of punishing the natives; their focus needed to remain on Rome.

"We're not attacking the natives of these lands," Boudica said, her voice loud and firm.

The men turned, stiffening at the sight of her.

"Verulamium is populated by native traitors who sided with the Romans," Gael said, glaring at her.

"That doesn't matter. This fight is against the Roman invaders, not against fellow tribes."

"I am chieftain of my tribe. I may have agreed to join you, but I take orders from no one," Gael growled, stepping toward her. He was tall, but their heights were evenly matched, and she didn't back away as he approached.

"Step back from my chieftain," Judoc hissed from behind her, moving to stand at her side, along with two of her guards.

"Tell your chieftain I don't take orders from her," Gael said, his eyes still trained on Boudica's, flashing with hostility.

The other warriors had noticed the growing conflict, and a hush fell over the camp. *Show him that he does take orders from you,* the dark voice whispered. *You are the leader of this army.*

But she ignored the dark whisper.

"We need not fight among each other. We agreed to work together. We have one common enemy; the Roman usurpers, not the natives of these lands."

"I told you; I don't take orders from you. And you're not one to speak of native traitors. You met with that traitor queen, Cartimandua. She's spread her legs for every Roman official who's come to these lands. How do we know you won't also become a Roman whore?" Gael spat.

Fury coursed through her, but before she could react, Judoc struck him. Her guards—and several of her warriors—lunged forward, tackling Gael and his men to the ground, pummeling them with their fists. Other warriors soon joined the fight, and Boudica stumbled back, panicked.

Cadell approached the mass of fighting men, shouting for calm, but they ignored him. More warriors were joining the fight; soon the mass of fighting bodies would be impossible to stop.

Boudica thought quickly, picking up a stray stick from the ground and lighting it from the flames of a nearby bonfire. She placed it on the ground, just a hairbreadth away from the fighting men. It ignited, flaring into a fire.

Gael and a dozen other men scrambled back. Two attendants rushed forward with a barrel of water, putting out the fire before it could spread farther, but the fire had already distracted most of the men enough from fighting.

"Are you mad?" Gael hissed. "You could have killed us all!"

"You're going to get yourselves killed if you keep fighting among each other," Boudica snapped. She raised her voice so that it could carry to the others. "This rebellion is not about taking orders, or infighting, or killing natives! Do you know what will happen if the Romans defeat us? There will be no mercy. They will kill us, burn down our villages and take us as slaves. If you're willing to sacrifice your freedom—and the freedom of your people—over petty differences, then leave this army and fight on your own!"

She met each man's gaze in silent challenge, but no one budged.

"We march on Verulamium at first light. And when we do, remember what we *truly* fight for."

When Boudica and her army descended upon Verulamium the next day, her worries about the infighting among the tribes had dissipated; she was only focused on victory. An uneasy peace had settled over the army after the brawl, and Gael had even offered her a gruff apology for his words, though she suspected that was because of Cadell and Judoc's firm insistence.

Now, she leapt into the center of fighting bodies,

clashing with a Roman soldier as they whirled and parried, until she stabbed him clean through.

Up ahead, Cadell stabbed a soldier, piercing his neck with a dagger, but he was charged from behind by another soldier before Boudica could shout a warning.

Judoc leapt onto the soldier, tearing him away from Cadell and breaking his neck. Cadell gave him a nod of thanks before charging forward.

Boudica whirled to face a soldier who darted toward her, his eyes burning with rage. This one was faster than the last, parrying each of her blows, and in a quick movement, he stabbed her in her side.

Pain seared her, hot and intense, and she stumbled back as he reared forward to deal a fatal blow, but she evaded, reaching out to stab her sword into the bare flesh of his leg. He sank to his knees, howling in agony, as yet another Roman soldier charged at her from behind.

She only barely managed to parry, growing weak from her wound, but she lurched forward, and with the last of her strength stabbed him in the throat. He slumped dead to the ground, blood seeping from his open wound.

Reeling from her bleeding side, Boudica stumbled forward, trying to staunch the bleeding with her hand. Warriors had set fire to many of the buildings, and it was increasingly difficult to see through the smoke-clogged streets as buildings burned around her.

She moved forward through the haze, coughing as she clutched her side, swaying on her feet. But she stilled when she heard the unmistakable screams of a family.

The smoke before her cleared, and she saw several warriors setting fire to several native roundhouses. Inside, the trapped residents screamed. The warriors pulled the surviving residents from their homes and strangled or stabbed them straight through with their swords.

Whirling, she noticed that behind her, warriors from her army were fighting each other. They strangled and stabbed, howling tribal cries as they did so.

Anger and disbelief spiraled through her. She opened her mouth to demand that they all stop, but she was too weak.

She gripped the side of a Roman building as she again swayed on her feet, but she couldn't hold herself upright, and succumbed to the void of darkness that claimed her.

IV

60 CE

The Iron Queen

23

Britannic countryside
Northwest of Verulamium

Suetonius rode away from the fort just after first light, only taking Aelius and a small contingent of soldiers with him. He'd not told them where they were going, and they'd followed without question.

He'd not slept much the previous night, not with Cartimandua's words floating through his mind, along with worried thoughts over his status in Rome. He had no doubt that word of the rebellion had reached Rome. The gossiping senators and Nero's advisors were probably enjoying his misfortune in Britannia. He'd gained many enemies as he rose through the ranks, enemies jealous of a mere soldier who'd risen to become praetor—then governor—of two provinces. He could imagine their whispered words, words they would make certain reached Nero's ears.

I heard he was starting to sympathize with the barbarians. There are some who say he willingly allowed the province to fall. He should be returned to Rome and executed for treason.

Unable to sleep, he'd gotten up and paced the wooden floors of his private quarters, looking out the window at the surrounding barracks, until his heart hardened and his resolve returned.

And that was when he'd had his revelation.

Now, he rode his horse to a wide field that slanted uphill, edged on the north side by a sprawling forest. He took it in for a long moment, a surge of hope filling him.

"Governor?" Aelius asked tentatively.

Suetonius turned to look back at Aelius and his weary men; their shadowed eyes, their fatigued faces.

Britannia was not a desired outpost for most soldiers. It was cold, gray and prone to rain, and there were rebellious tribes to contend with. Many of them had lost friends in the recent barbarian uprising. They'd also received word from their scouts that Tertius had been among the Romans killed at Verulamium; it had been yet another demoralizing blow.

Regret spiraled through him; he'd not been a good leader to them during this uprising, focused on his own self-reproach. But that would change. If they were to overcome the odds to defeat the massive barbarian army, he would have to be the leader they deserved.

"The barbarians have used surprise tactics to their advantage," he said, his voice loud enough to carry to each man.

"And their numbers," Aelius grumbled.

"Their numbers can be their detriment. I've fought many campaigns against barbarians, and I've noticed one commonality; they use chaos as their weapon. Disorder. But *we* fight as one—that has always been our strength. We have discipline. Unity. Order. They do not. We need to take advantage of their chaos, their usual advantage of surprise. We'll let them find us. But this time . . . we pick where we fight."

He turned, gesturing to the sloping field.

"This will be the place."

He'd passed by this area years before, when he'd marched west for a campaign. He'd remembered the sloping field edged by trees, and his soldier's mind knew it would make a perfect defensive location.

"The barbarians will surge toward us, having to climb uphill. We will have to do nothing but push forward, allowing the massive army to collapse in on itself. It is a risk, but the barbarians are not disciplined enough to hold off their attack. Their lack of discipline has always been their downfall."

Now there was a flicker of hope on some of the men's faces, though others still looked uncertain.

"Their numbers could still overwhelm us, Governor. I told you what I witnessed at Camulodunum—and that was when their army was smaller. I think we should hold off until more soldiers can join us. There's another fort north where we can regroup and hold off the barbarian army until—" Aelius began.

"The barbarian army will arrive before more legions do," Suetonius said bluntly. "The scouts tell us their camp is not far south from here. They'd surround us and attack. Our best chance of victory is to bring the barbarians to us." He raised his voice to address the other men. "Return to the fort, prepare the other men. We ride tomorrow at first light."

As the men turned and rode away, he gestured for Aelius to approach.

"I want to arrange a meeting with the barbarian queen who leads the rebels. Boudica."

Aelius paled, his eyes going wide.

This had been the second part of his revelation. He'd kept thinking about Cartimandua's words, that he could reason with the Icenian queen. He doubted this, but a meeting with her could buy their army some much needed time. And . . . he wanted to speak to his foe out of morbid curiosity, this woman who'd succeeded in ways others before her had failed. He'd always been an expert at reading his enemies, and if he met her face-to-face, he could surmise what her weaknesses were . . . weaknesses he could use to kill her on the battlefield.

"Governor, I must protest," Aelius sputtered.

"The barbarian queen is mad. You don't mean to reason with—"

"A meeting will give us more time to prepare for battle, and we need as much time as we can gain. Send a messenger to the barbarian camp to arrange the meeting. That is an order," Suetonius said, his tone firm.

He turned his horse and rode back toward the fort, but not before casting one last glance back at the sloping field. It was here that he prayed Fortuna would smile down upon him and his men and grant them a victory to crush Boudica and her barbarian army.

24

Prasutagus held her in his arms, and Boudica leaned into his familiar, comforting warmth. They were back in their home, seated before the hearth. He stroked her hair as he gazed down at her, his amber eyes filled with love.

"Husband," she whispered, her voice breaking as she reached up to trace the features of the face she loved so much. "I miss you."

"And I you, wife," he murmured, capturing her hand in his and pressing it to his lips. "But you must wake up. Our daughters need you. Our people need you."

Tears blurred her eyes; she wanted to tell him that she needed him. He seemed to read her thoughts and gave her a sad smile before leaning forward to press his lips to hers.

Boudica awoke with a start. She was lying on an animal pelt on the edge of the army's camp, while a healer tended to her wound. Kensa and Mael hovered above her, their expressions tight with worry. Fierce pain shot through her, and she grimaced, but attempted to sit up.

"No," Kensa said firmly. "The healer still tends to your wound. You must remain still. Here."

Kensa gave Boudica a handful of valerian root, and she nibbled on it, taking deep breaths to ease her pain. The healer bound her side with tartan fabric, then handed her a jug of water. Boudica forced the water down in several swallows.

"How long since the battle?" she asked, setting down the jug and looking around. The army had set up camp in the surrounding fields outside of Verulamium, which lay in ruins in the distance. The crackle of bonfires and rumble of voices from the army filled the camp, the gaiety in the air a contrast to the violence she'd witnessed before succumbing to her wound.

"The battle ended at midday; night has just fallen," Mael replied.

"My daughters?" she asked Kensa.

"They're fine. Playing with the other children," Kensa assured her. "They're worried about you, but I told them you're being tended to."

Kensa leaned forward to help her sit up, and Boudica propped herself up against a log that an attendant had covered with more animal pelts. The valerian Kensa had given her was already working, the pain in her side subsiding to a dull ache.

"I need to speak with the other chieftains," she said, looking up at Mael, her expression darkening as she recalled what she'd seen at Verulamium; the screams of natives as her army killed them, the infighting among her own men.

Mael's eyes met hers and he gave her a nod, seeming to already understand the reason for her dark expression. Kensa helped her stand, though she insisted Boudica needed more rest, but left as the other chieftains approached.

"You're awake," Gael observed; he looked mildly disappointed. "We feared you'd joined the gods."

"I'll not die until the Romans are gone from these lands," she said, giving him a hard stare. "I thought it was understood our fight is with Rome. Why were our men attacking the natives?"

"The army is thousands strong," Corentin said. "Our word can only carry to so many."

"And many in the army can't distinguish between the Verulamium natives and the Romans. They bed the Romans, speak their language, and fight against other native tribes on behalf of Rome," Gael said tightly.

"None of that matters in *our* fight," Boudica hissed. "And what of our men fighting with each other? We agreed to work together."

"Corentin is right. An army of this size is difficult to control," Cadell said. "Animosities run deep between some tribes, animosities that are difficult to put aside."

"I told you all—we need to fight in unison," Boudica said, frustration roiling through her. "We can't continue to—"

"We've been victorious, destroying their settlements with the Romans on the run," Yannik interjected. "Disagreements among the tribes haven't hindered us."

"They will if they continue," Boudica returned, clutching her side as a sudden wave of pain swept over her. "We need to gather our men and explain that—"

The frantic cries of a man behind her interrupted her words. Boudica turned as Judoc dragged a Roman messenger toward her. He threw the messenger to the ground at her feet.

"This filth was skulking outside our camp."

The messenger remained kneeling, looking down at the ground as he addressed them.

"I am here on behalf of Governor Suetonius Paulinus. He wishes to meet with Queen Boudica. In —in private."

Judoc let out a snort of disbelief.

"Where do you want me to kill him?"

"No—please! I beg you—" the messenger sputtered.

"Wait," Boudica said, holding her hand up to Judoc and stepping forward. "What does he want to discuss?"

"Boudica, this filth doesn't—" Judoc began.

"Let him answer."

"He—he wishes to discuss a possible truce. An end to the bloodshed."

Boudica approached her horse on the edge of camp, trailed by Judoc, two of her guards, and Kensa. Mael, Cadell and the other chieftains had tried to dissuade her from meeting with the governor; Corentin had offered to go in her stead. But with the dark look in Corentin's eyes, she'd refused. Corentin —or any of the other chieftains, including Cadell— would likely kill the governor on sight.

She'd met Suetonius before, when he'd come to the village for diplomatic meetings with Prasutagus. Unlike Catus, who looked at her and the other natives as if they were rodents, Suetonius treated the villagers with something akin to respect. She hoped that he was a Roman she could reason with.

Kensa stepped forward, wrapping a tartan cloak around her, which Boudica lifted to cover her head.

"You don't have to do this," Kensa said in a low voice, as Judoc and her guards mounted their horses. "How do you know he won't capture you and take you back to Rome in chains?"

"We're meeting right outside of camp. If it's an ambush, we'll have the whole of our army on him."

"And I'd rip the head from his body if he tried," Judoc grumbled.

But Kensa still looked concerned.

"Why can't you speak through messengers?"

"There's no time . . . we've decided to march at first light. And I won't show cowardice by refusing to meet with him. He needs to know we stand firm."

She gave Kensa a nod of farewell and turned her horse to ride away from camp, trailing the Roman messenger. The messenger had told her Suetonius was just north of their camp with only a handful of men with him.

They soon arrived at a small patch of forest where two Roman soldiers stood guard. Alarm filled her at the sight, but the soldiers only gave her curt nods, though there was hot contempt in their eyes, before they turned to lead her and her guards into the forest.

Suetonius stood in a moonlit-dappled clearing before a trickling stream. To her surprise, he was alone. He was taller than she'd remembered and had the look of a seasoned soldier: tall and muscular, his dark hair cropped close to his scalp, his skin browned from marching and fighting beneath an unrelenting sun.

"Queen Boudica." His voice was deep and booming; it reminded her of her father's: a voice used to commanding armies. His eyes strayed to Judoc and her guards. "Thank you for meeting me. May I speak with you alone?"

Boudica dismissed Judoc and her guards with a wave; they looked hesitant but obliged.

"We'll be just beyond the clearing," Judoc said,

his voice sharp with warning and loud enough for Suetonius to hear.

Once they were alone, Boudica's gaze strayed to the stream Suetonius stood before. Votive offerings filled it; statues of gods and goddesses. Suetonius followed her gaze.

"Those are offerings from the tribes of these lands to their gods," she said, when he followed her gaze. "They pray for the fall of Rome. So they may live in peace."

Suetonius's jaw tightened.

"Peace is what everyone wants, regardless of where they are born, the ruler they follow, the gods they worship."

"Rome doesn't want peace," she returned. "It just wants . . . more. More land, more slaves, more bloodshed in its name."

Something unreadable flared in his eyes. Agreement? Sympathy? But the look was gone as quickly as it appeared.

"It is what I want," he said finally. "It is what your husband wanted. Your father as well."

Hot anger seized her, and she took a breath to keep her voice steady.

"And they were both slain. By their Roman 'allies.'"

"I assure you, Catus's actions were not at the behest of Rome, but his own greed. I was disgusted by what he did to you and your daughters. He remained in Londinium to face you on my orders. He would have fled otherwise," he said, probing her eyes, a look of apology in his own.

Astonishment struck her; she'd never seen a Roman official look apologetic for anything.

"You expect my gratitude?" she asked, setting her astonishment aside.

"I only want to show that I can be reasonable. I am not Catus. He let his greed rule him."

"And what rules you?"

"Loyalty. Duty."

"To Rome. To your emperor," she spat.

"Yes. I do not deny it. Even though . . . I have not always agreed with their tactics."

A brief shadow appeared on his face and surprise coursed through her once more. She was used to Romans such as Catus, who wore their black hearts with pride. Suetonius seemed more . . . human.

"The empire has created order when before there was none," he said now. "Civilization."

"Your *empire* has created fear and destruction. If that's 'civilization,' my people and I want no part of it."

"Queen Boudica," Suetonius said, his voice tight, "your tribe has been allies with Rome for nearly twenty years. Surely you don't want to end such a peace."

"There was never peace, only forced submission. Now we just want our freedom."

"If you stop this rebellion now, I can plead to Emperor Nero for mercy on your behalf. Negotiate a way for your people to keep your lands," Suetonius said as if she hadn't spoken at all.

"Both my husband and my father trusted the word of a Roman . . . now they're both dead. There will be no more alliances."

Suetonius's expression hardened. He took a step forward, and though he was taller than her, one of the few men who were, she didn't flinch, and evenly met his gaze.

"This rebellion will not end well for you nor your people," he hissed. "Even if you defeat my legions, do you think Emperor Nero would allow a woman to usurp him? His pride would never allow that. *Rome* would never allow that. I know my brethren well, and let me tell you this—they are used to victory. They will not relent. They will brutalize your people into submission. I'm offering you a way out."

His expression softened as his gaze probed hers; she was unnerved by the lack of spite in his eyes, the lack of dismissive rage she'd seen so often in Catus's.

But submission was not an option. She wasn't naïve enough to believe that the Romans would leave her and her people in peace after the rebellion. There was no turning back, not until she fulfilled the promise she'd made to her daughters and her people, that she would keep fighting until the Romans left their lands.

"We've killed thousands of your brethren and razed three of your settlements, including your capital. Your threats mean nothing. I'll offer *you* a way out. If you and your men leave our lands, I'll help with your safe passage. But if your men stay—or return—we'll show no mercy. And you know what my army is capable of."

"Do you know how many self-righteous leaders like you that I've defeated?" Suetonius spat. "This is no different. You are no different."

"You act like you are above the evil the Romans have committed. But you are one and the same . . . chained to your precious empire like a slave."

Suetonius flinched; she was pleased that her words had affected him.

"We want you off of our lands," she continued, her eyes hard. "We can be just as relentless as your empire."

"Very well. It is a shame, as a part of me admires you, as foolish as you are. I will tell you this," he continued, lowering his voice. He leaned in, intimately close. "My face will be the last you see before you die."

"Or will it be the other way around?" Boudica returned, ignoring the dread that flowed through her at his words. "I have killed many Romans. I will be glad to send one more to his gods."

Suetonius's eyes filled with fire, and his mouth twisted in a humorless smile.

"I look forward to seeing who is right," he murmured. "I will see you on the battlefield, Queen Boudica."

25

When Boudica returned to camp, chaos had descended. Two separate fights had broken out among warriors of two different tribes. She dismounted from her horse and rushed to Mael's side, who watched with a tumultuous expression as Cadell, Judoc and a dozen other warriors broke up the mass of fighting bodies.

"What happened?" Boudica demanded.

"A combat challenge descended into this," Mael said, gesturing to the fighting men with a scowl.

Unease spiraled through her as the fighting warriors were separated. Tomorrow they were to fight a trained, unified Roman army, and her army still fought among themselves.

"What did the Roman governor say?" Mael asked, studying her taut features.

"Many things," Boudica said, expelling a shaky sigh. "I need to meet with the other chieftains."

Moments later, Boudica stood opposite Cadell and the other chieftains on the edge of camp.

"The Romans will not relent," she told them. "The governor is determined to take back Britannia."

"He's frightened of us," Yannik said. "He tried to intimidate you because you're a woman. He should have met with one of us."

"Then the bastard would no longer have his head," Gael growled.

"You *must* tell your men to heed orders and to stop fighting among themselves," Boudica snapped. "The Romans fight as one. We do not. What happened at Verulamium—warriors turning on each other—it can't happen again."

"We don't fight like the Romans, we fight like men," Corentin said with a scowl. "And we will continue to do so."

"Burning down Roman settlements and overtaking smaller contingents of Roman soldiers isn't the same as pitched battle," Boudica said, her frustration rising. "Tomorrow's battle is different—our scouts tell us the governor has called all the remaining Roman soldiers to fight as one. Rome has yet to send more soldiers, the nearest legions are embroiled in other conflicts and won't get here in time. If we defeat them, these lands will be ours. Then we can fight off any other soldiers they send."

"We'll defeat them," Yannik said calmly. "Our numbers will overwhelm them. I'll speak to my men —but I'll not caution them. I'll tell them to continue to fight as they have been, and to kill as many Romans as they can."

"Boudica speaks the truth," Cadell interjected, leveling each chieftain with a glare. "We must plan, focus, and—"

"Our men are our own, and we are the ones who give them orders," Gael snapped, his eyes narrowed. "We fight with you, *Queen* Boudica," he continued, spitting the word "queen". "Not for you."

"I want victory for us all. I want freedom for us all," Boudica insisted.

"As do we," Gael returned.

"Then urge your men to obey orders and fight as one. And . . ." She hesitated, but forced herself to continue, "because tomorrow's battle is different, your warriors may want to send their families away for protection."

"Families have traveled with us from the start," Yannik said with a fierce scowl, shaking his head. "My men will want them to watch us take our victory."

"It seems like you're not preparing for victory, but for defeat," Gael growled, stepping forward. "Tonight, my men will feast and bed their wives. Tomorrow they'll march with their families at the rear, as they've always done, and watch as we destroy the last of the Roman vermin."

He gave her one last defiant glare before turning to leave, trailed by the other chieftains.

"Chieftains are more stubborn than most,"

Cadell muttered as they walked away. "I will have Mael and the other priests speak to them."

Boudica nodded, though she was unconvinced that anything Mael could say would sway them.

But she knew what she needed to do—for her and her daughters.

"Perhaps I shouldn't say this to the leader of the army," Elouan said, with a hesitant smile. "But after the rebellion, I'll be happy to put my sword down."

Boudica smiled. "It is my hope as well."

She sat next to her daughters and opposite Elouan and Kensa over their personal bonfire. She'd had an attendant prepare as fine a dinner as she could muster from their provisions; charred pork and bread, and sweet mead her army had taken from the stores in Verulamium. In the time between battles, there had been no time for fine dinners; Kensa and her daughters had looked delighted at the sight of the prepared meal.

Boudica drank in their happiness. There had been little joy among them since Prasutagus's death. She decided not to tell them the true reason for the fine dinner, not until later. For now, she wanted to enjoy this time with her girls and her oldest friend. She'd invited Elouan as well; he was a part of her plan.

She'd watched him interact with Kensa and her daughters during the meal; he had an easy camaraderie with each of them. They all listened intently as he spoke of his father, who'd been a craftsman as well and taught him the trade. He'd learned to fight like other young men in the tribe, but the only true fighting he'd done had been during the recent battles.

"I will have a wife to look after," he was saying now, and gave Kensa a look which made her blush. Kensa looked at Boudica, her face flushed with happiness.

"I've accepted Elouan's proposal. We'll wed after the fighting is done," she said. "With your permission, of course."

Boudica reached out to squeeze her friend's hand, glad to see her so happy.

"Of course," she said.

"Mama, I've been working on the tale of the rebellion with the bards," Nolwenn said eagerly. "Can I tell it to you?"

Brighid let out a playful groan.

"She's told us this tale too many times."

"I'll be happy to hear it," Boudica said, smiling.

Nolwenn shot her sister an annoyed glance, straightening her tunic as she stood, facing them all. She schooled her expression into a grave one, an expression Boudica had seen on the faces of the bards before they launched into their tales.

"There lives a beast called Rome. A savage and ravenous beast, Rome has conquered most of the known world. It has turned hungry eyes across the great waters, to the wild lands of the north . . . to the lands they call Britannia. But Rome would create a beast of its own making, one that would cripple the knees of the mighty empire. Her name is Boudica, chieftain of the Iceni."

Nolwenn continued the tale, her voice rising and falling with dramatic flourish. As Boudica listened to Nolwenn's tale of her army destroying three Roman settlements, her chest filled with turmoil, because she didn't know how this story would end. *With victory,* she prayed. *Please, Andraste. Bless our army with victory tomorrow.*

When Nolwenn finished her tale with dramatic relish, Boudica grinned and clapped, along with Kensa and Elouan.

"Do you like it?" Nolwenn asked, suddenly looking shy.

"Yes. Very much," Boudica said, pulling Nolwenn into her lap with a loving smile. She turned to face Brighid, still smiling. "I've seen you practice fighting with the other children. Will you show me some of what you've learned?"

It was Brighid's turn to look shy. She looked at Kensa, who gave her an encouraging nod, before clambering to her feet.

Boudica and Brighid found two sticks nearby and sparred as the others watched. Though her daughter's movements were shaky and unskilled, Boudica could see the raw natural talent she had, and pride swelled within her. She would make a fine warrior one day.

After Boudica and Brighid completed their sparring, they all shared the rest of the mead and bread. Boudica tried to remember every detail of these moments; the firelight dancing off her daughters' smiling faces, Kensa's laughter, her hand entwined with Elouan's, her head resting on his shoulder.

But as the attendants came to take the remnants of their food away, Boudica knew it was time to reveal what she'd truly brought them here for. She stood and gave them a forced smile.

"Let's walk. The night is beautiful."

Kensa looked puzzled as Boudica took her daughters by the hand. She led them all away from camp, entering the sprawling forest that surrounded it.

"Your father and I played in forests like these when we were children," she said, a sudden wave of nostalgia and longing for Prasutagus sweeping over her.

"At night?" Nolwenn asked.

"Sometimes. I've always loved the forest. I've always felt . . . free here. When I was a girl, I could practice fight in the forest without being scolded by Rozen. Sometimes Aunt Kensa stood guard outside the trees."

She glanced behind her at Kensa with a small smile. But Kensa looked uneasy, and Boudica suspected she'd guessed her intentions.

Boudica stopped at a clearing, kneeling down before Brighid and Nolwenn.

"I never thought I'd have daughters of my own," she whispered. "I didn't realize how fiercely I could love until I birthed both of you."

She reached out to touch their faces, trying to memorize every detail of their features.

"Your father didn't want me to start this uprising. I broke my vow to him . . . for the both of you. For our people. But your father had another desire, one we both share. He wanted you both to live a long and happy life. For this final battle, I'm sending you both away," Boudica forced herself to say. "Your Aunt Kensa—and Elouan, if he chooses—is going with you."

A stunned silence followed her words. At the edge of the clearing, Kensa went stiff with alarm, while Elouan widened his eyes with surprise.

Brighid looked at her in angry shock; Nolwenn's eyes filled with tears.

"Why, Mama?" Nolwenn whispered.

"Tomorrow's battle . . . it's not like the others. Their numbers may be small, but it's the largest army of Romans we've fought against. The fighting will be especially brutal and fierce. It's not safe for you to be near."

"But Uncle Judoc says we're winning," Brighid protested.

"We are," Boudica assured her. "I'm just being careful. You're the daughters of the chief rebel. If we're defeated, the Romans would make an example out of you. And I promised you both I'd never let anyone harm you again."

"But you won't be defeated," Brighid said fiercely. "Our army is winning, and we—"

"My decision is final," Boudica said, her voice steady and firm. "There's a tribe in the far north untouched by Rome, the Caledonians. They're allies; the chieftain was a friend to my father. They'll take you in. I'll join you after the battle."

Before her dinner with the girls and Kensa, she'd spoken to Mael, asking him if their tribe had any alliances with distant tribes unaffected by Rome.

"The Caledonians in the far north," Mael had replied. "We used to trade with them. Your father was friends with the chief before he was forced to ally with Rome."

"Do you think they would take in my daughters?"

"The Caledonians hate the Romans. For rising against Rome, I have no doubt you're a goddess in their eyes. I know many people of the tribe; they are good people. They will happily take in your daughters"

"No. Mama, let me stay and fight. Please—" Brighid was saying now, her green eyes filling with tears.

"No, Brighid. You will go north with your sister where it's safe."

"Then promise you'll join us," Brighid said, searching her eyes.

"I can't promise that," Boudica said. "Every battle is uncertain, but I will try—"

"Promise us!" Brighid interrupted, her voice cracking. "Promise! Promise! Promise—"

Boudica silenced her by reaching out to pull her into her arms. She stroked her daughter's hair, closing her eyes, her heart splintering in her chest.

"I can't, my love. But I will try to return to you. You, Nolwenn and your father . . . you're my great loves. But I started this fight. I have to finish it."

She reached for Nolwenn, and both daughters wept in her arms. She held them close until their tears dissolved, looking up over their heads at Kensa. Kensa stood still and silent, with Elouan tightly gripping her hand, though tears streamed down her face.

Boudica forced herself to release her daughters, looking down at them with a resolve she didn't feel.

"You have a long journey ahead," she said, her voice wavering. "You need to be on your way."

She turned to a cluster of trees behind her, waving toward two guards and an attendant who'd been waiting out of sight behind them. They emerged from the trees, pulling two horse-driven carts loaded with belongings.

Kensa and her daughters' eyes widened with surprise. The attendant stepped forward, taking Nolwenn by her hand. Brighid stepped back, and Boudica feared she would put up a fight. But she reluctantly allowed the attendant to take her hand.

Boudica reached down to embrace her daughters once more, burying her face in their hair.

"Always know how much I love you," she whispered.

They met her eyes, their own glistening with tears, as the attendant led them away.

Boudica turned to Kensa, who'd gone pale, and Elouan.

"Elouan," she said, trying to keep her voice level. "If you do not wish to leave—"

"My home is with Kensa," he said, squeezing Kensa's hand. Kensa smiled as he lifted her hand to his lips. He then left them to approach the horses, as if sensing they needed time alone.

"You don't have to do this," Kensa whispered, stepping forward. "Come with us. No one'll fault you for wanting to be with your girls. You've led the tribes farther than anyone has in a rebellion."

"I have to finish this," Boudica interrupted. She stepped forward, gripping Kensa's shaking hands. "If —if I don't survive—"

"Don't say—"

"If I don't," Boudica continued, firm, "take care of my girls. I think Elouan would make a good father to them."

Her voice trembled, and she had to blink back another wave of tears as she pulled Kensa into a firm embrace.

"You're my sister. I love you fiercely."

Kensa closed her eyes, her shoulders shaking with

silent sobs as they held each other for several long moments. Boudica rested her forehead against Kensa's before stepping back.

"Tomorrow . . . kill them all," Kensa said, her voice laced with ferocity, even as her eyes shone with tears. "And then come for your daughters, and raise them to become fierce women like you."

With those words, Kensa turned and joined Elouan and her daughters, climbing onto the cart next to them. They all faced her as the horse pulled them away, keeping their gazes trained on her face.

Boudica kept watching them, with tears in her eyes, until they faded from view through the trees.

26

Boudica knelt before Mael, her eyes closed as he smeared the blood of a slain boar on her forehead. She sat in a semicircle with Judoc, Cadell, and the other chieftains as Mael blessed them before the day's battle.

It was just after dawn, and sunlight bathed the camp and surrounding countryside in varying shades of yellow and white light; it seemed as if the gods were highlighting the lands they fought for.

"Gods, we call on you now, to stand with us on the battlefield, to guide us to victory, to purge the wicked from our lands," Mael intoned, his voice carrying above the chirp of early morning birds, the whisper of the morning breeze. "To allow us to dwell in peace on the lands you have blessed us with, free of Roman tyranny."

Other groups of warriors knelt in semicircles throughout the camp as druid priests blessed them before the battle. There was a hushed silence over the camp, and though the warriors still displayed great confidence, they were all aware of the significance of the upcoming battle. It wasn't the mere destruction of a Roman settlement and the soldiers who tried to defend it; this battle was a direct confrontation with the men who'd usurped their lands.

After Mael concluded the prayers, her attendant helped her prepare, painting her face and arm with tribal tattoos. Today, Boudica had pinned two brooches to her tunic; one was the horse brooch her father had given her years ago, the other a gift from Prasutagus.

Would they be proud of her, her husband and father? Would they be worried? She suspected they would feel a little of both.

I'll make you proud, she thought, imagining them standing before her. *Even if you fear for me, even if I am defeated, I will make you proud.*

She thought of her daughters, now making their way north. She smiled as she recalled Nolwenn's tale of Boudica and her rebellion. A pang pierced her; she already missed her daughters and prayed she could join them, to return to their village as a people free of the Romans. She tried not to let herself think of defeat, but the knowledge that her daughters were far from the reach of the Romans comforted her.

The army congregated just north of their camp, ready to march, and she mounted her horse to ride out to the head of the army, joining the other chieftains. The warriors of the massive army were no longer silent, bellowing prayers to the gods and triumphant battle cries, ready to seize their victory.

When Boudica spoke, a sense of calm had settled over her, and unlike the first time she had to address her army, she knew exactly what to say.

"They've tried to beat us into submission, to break who we are!" she shouted, her voice carrying over their frenzied cries. "But every wrong they've committed against us—the starvation, the rape, the murder, the slavery—we've returned it tenfold with the destruction of their settlements and the slaughter of their men. Their wrongdoing has led us to this day, to this battle . . . to victory! To the freedom we've prayed for. To the freedom we've fought for!"

The battle cries soared. She turned to Cadell and Judoc, who rode at her side. Judoc gave her a wide grin, Cadell a nod of assured confidence, and she turned her horse, leading her army to what she prayed was victory.

THEY MARCHED NORTH FOR SOME TIME BEFORE spotting the Roman army in the distance. They stood in wedge formation on the top of a small hill. Though her army far outnumbered theirs, a trickle of unease filled her at the sight of the Roman army's uphill position, at their unmoving bodies, which remained still even as her massive army approached.

"Look at their numbers," Gael snorted at her side. "A few thousand at most. We have tens of thousands. Looks like we've killed most of the Roman rats. This'll be over before midday."

Yet Boudica didn't feel such certainty. She surveyed the battlefield: the sloping hillside and the trees at the back of the Roman army. She turned, glancing back at her army. Though it was great in number, it was unwieldy. At the rear of the army, she could make out specks of the families of warriors who rode in carts and wagons, shouting encouragements and tribal battle cries.

Boudica turned, stopping her horse a few hundred yards away from the Roman lines. Behind her, her army shouted and hissed at the Roman soldiers, who remained still and stoic behind their shields. Boudica searched the front lines, finally spotting Suetonius standing to the side of his soldiers, his hard gaze trained on her. She recalled his words with a chill. *This rebellion will not end well for you.*

Boudica turned to Cadell, her heart hammering.

"We need to surround them."

Cadell nodded his agreement. She turned her horse to face her unwieldy army, shouting above their battle cries.

"On my command, we must—"

But her words were lost among the excitement and fury of the thousands behind her. They took her words to mean that they must charge, and before she could complete her order, they charged forward, bellowing out even more battle cries as they surged toward the Roman lines.

"Spread out! Surround them!" Boudica cried.

But her words were still lost amid the frenzy. The massive forward surge of bodies swept her along, and she had to dismount from her horse to avoid falling and being crushed.

She took out her sword, charging toward the Roman lines. The Romans remained unmoving, even as her army charged toward them. Boudica kept racing forward with her army, moving uphill to meet them, but still the Romans did not move, and her army clashed into the Romans with sheer, brute force, man against man, skin against armor.

For several long moments, a stalemate stretched as Boudica pushed and heaved against the Romans along with her army, trying to get them to budge, but they still would not move.

Ice filled her veins when she heard Suetonius's voice, firm and commanding, bellow, "Weapons!"

Moving as one, the Romans drew their short swords.

"Forward!"

Maintaining their wedge formation, the Romans surged forward, thrusting out with their swords as they moved, pushing back against her massive army.

Boudica realized with growing horror that the force of the wedge formation was savagely effective as the Romans moved forward, stabbing the mass of native fighters, forcing them downhill. The sheer size of the tribal army quickly became a detriment as they fell back and crushed each other.

"Get to your feet! Push forward!" Boudica cried.

Around her, some warriors did manage to break through the fierce wedge of Romans, weapons at the ready, killing any soldier in their path, but most of the warriors continued to be pushed back by the Roman surge, stabbed and crushed by the relentless push of the Roman soldiers.

Boudica forced herself forward, successfully slashing at various Roman soldiers with her sword as she moved past their lines. Through the mass of bodies, she could see Cadell doing the same, shouting to other warriors around him to keep moving forward.

But the Romans had already made significant progress, continuing to push the army downhill. Boudica watched in dazed disbelief as scores of warriors around her fell—either trampled or stabbed by the Romans and their swords.

She continued to charge forward, heart hammering, stabbing as many soldiers as she could. Others, including Judoc, followed her lead, forcibly pushing past the Roman lines, cutting down soldiers as they darted forward.

One Roman soldier charged toward her with his sword outstretched, but she stabbed him through before whirling to clash with another soldier. After she slew him, sending him to the ground screaming with a bleeding throat, her eyes found Suetonius, only yards away from her as he stabbed a native warrior straight through with his sword.

She charged toward him, and Suetonius whirled as she approached, their swords clashing in midair. He met her eyes as they began to fight, their swords meeting in rapid-fire moves. Boudica stepped back and lunged forward, aiming for his throat, but Suetonius parried. He darted forward, aiming for her heart, but she parried as well. He didn't wait to charge forward again, and before Boudica could parry once more, his sword pierced the flesh of her abdomen, reopening the old wound she'd received in Verulamium. He continued to thrust forward, his hard eyes on her, as he sank the sword deep into her stomach.

The moment seemed suspended in time, a long and darkly intimate moment as his dark eyes locked with hers, holding the sword in her abdomen. She thought she might have seen a brief flicker of regret in his dark eyes before the look was gone.

Pain like she had never known tore through her, its tendrils curling around every part of her body, and a chilling cold seeped into her veins. Hot moisture dripped from her mouth, and she dimly realized that it was blood. Suetonius pulled his sword out of her flesh, keeping his eyes trained on hers.

Blood soaked her tunic, and she clutched at it, fighting to remain on her feet, but her sword had slipped from her hand. Suetonius stepped forward, his dark eyes hard and fierce, and she realized that he was going to deliver the final, killing blow—

But Cadell lunged at him from behind, and Suetonius whirled to fight him, their swords clashing.

Boudica looked down; her blood seeped from beneath her fingers, and she could no longer stand upright. She stumbled to her knees, her vision going dim as all around her, Roman soldiers slaughtered her army. They'd pushed much of her army downhill and back across the field, slaughtering all those who weren't trampled. In the distance, she heard the piercing screams of the families who'd watched the battle from the rear of the army. *The Romans are slaughtering them as well*, Boudica realized, with icy dread.

She saw a Roman soldier rush at Cadell from behind as he fought Suetonius. She wanted to shout out a warning, but she was too weak—and it was too late. As Cadell whirled, the Roman soldier stabbed him straight through the chest. Cadell's eyes widened as he went lifeless and slumped to the ground. She saw another Roman soldier stab Judoc straight through his chest, and Judoc sank to the ground and slumped over, his eyes wide and lifeless.

Deep beneath her pain, grief tore through her, and though she knew her army was suffering a crushing defeat, that she was dying, she struggled to maintain consciousness, to get to her feet and keep fighting.

Yet the world around her was fading. Someone

lifted her up, and she met Mael's eyes as he and another warrior carried her dying body off the battlefield. She fought to keep her eyes open, and through the midst of Roman soldiers slaughtering her brethren, she saw . . . Antedios.

He stood on the edge of the battlefield, giving her a sad but proud smile. Rozen stood next to him, her hand over her heart, her eyes brimming with tears. Boudica weakly returned their smiles, and a rush of warmth filled her as she saw another familiar face, this one standing in the center of the battlefield.

Her husband. Her beloved. Prasutagus. His smile was filled with tenderness and love.

I'm sorry I broke my promise. But our daughters are safe, she wanted to tell him, if she could speak. *I sent them away. They will live long and happy lives—what you wanted for them. What we both wanted for them.*

He merely gave her a nod, as if he understood . . . and was giving her permission to let go.

Boudica's breathing grew more ragged, yet she struggled to keep her gaze on his fading image.

She recalled their practice fights in the groves when they were young. His eyes filled with desire and love on their wedding day. Prasutagus sinking to his knees on the day she told him she was with child. She thought of their daughters: their screaming, red faces as they were born, the love that engulfed her as she held them in her arms for the first time.

And she thought of other times: sitting with Kensa before the hearth and sharing a cup of mead, Rozen telling her and Kensa stories as they drifted off to sleep on their bed furs, her father's face, gruff and emotional, as he gifted her with her mother's horse brooch.

When she was young, she'd wondered what warriors saw before they died and drifted from the land of the living to the land of the gods. Now she knew. After a life of violence and blood, their last moments were of love. The people they'd loved, the moments they'd spent with them. At the center of it all, warriors fought for what they loved.

And she'd loved her family, her people, her lands. It was this love she carried with her, as she slipped from the land of the living, like a leaf drifting from the branch of a tree.

Let go. Prasutagus's voice was faint, carrying to her from the land of the gods. *You have fought well, my love. Rest now. I will see you soon.*

Boudica's eyes drifted shut. Darkness—and peace—claimed her.

27

He couldn't find the queen.

After fighting off the barbarian fighter who'd prevented him from delivering another blow to Boudica, Suetonius had intended to finish her off with his sword, to see the defiant light in her eyes fade, but she was no longer on the battlefield.

And after his men had thoroughly defeated the barbarian army, he'd had his men scour the battlefield. Once, twice, three times.

Yet she was gone. He knew she couldn't have survived, the wound he'd given her was fatal, but he needed to see her dead body with his own eyes. And he knew Nero would have wanted to see it, to display her head in Rome and then to their various provinces for onlookers to gaze upon, evidence of Rome's might over those who dared to defy.

But there was something else that niggled at him.

As he'd delivered the fatal blow, his sword sinking into her flesh, a small flicker of regret darted through him, regret over striking down such a formidable foe, someone who looked at him with open defiance instead of submission and fear. Full-fledged fury now replaced his regret. Her surviving men must have carried her off for burial, to worship her like one of their gods. He wanted to obliterate her and her noble but failed cause. He didn't want those who'd survived to tell her tale, to make a martyr out of her, to keep telling her story long after she was gone. She was a fool: a defiant, brave fool who might have kept her life if only she'd listened to reason.

He pushed the thought aside, straightening as Aelius approached. She was gone, dead by his hand, and that was all that mattered. He'd make certain that her people—and the other people of this cursed island—knew to never defy Rome again. He would subdue them, even more brutally than before, without his conscience to nag at him. Their defiant leader was dead, and he would stamp out any remaining traces of rebellion.

"Governor," Aelius said, approaching. "We've begun digging mass graves for the dead."

"That can wait," Suetonius said, as he straightened. "Go after any fleeing survivors. Slaughter them and leave their bodies to rot where they can be seen."

Never would any barbarian defy Rome under his watch again.

Brighid sat cross-legged next to Nolwenn, warming her hands above the fire as they ate the charred meat their attendant had prepared. They were close to the lands of the Caledonian tribe, having traveled most of the day and night, stopping periodically to give the horses time to rest and eat.

During the journey, Aunt Kensa tried to look upbeat and cheerful. But her face was pale and taut with worry; Brighid knew that she feared for her mother. Nolwenn was more open with her worry, weeping every time they stopped for a break, pleading with the riders to stop and wait for their mother to join them.

But Brighid held her tears at bay, proud of herself for maintaining a brave façade. She was embarrassed by the weeping she'd done after leaving her mother the night before. When their mother joined them, she could tell her how strong she'd been, how she knew Boudica would join them. She smiled as she recalled sparring with her mother; one day she would be just as fine a warrior.

She stilled when she heard horse hooves and a rolling cart approaching behind them. Brighid beamed, scrambling to her feet and turning around.

But she froze at the sight of a somber-looking Mael, accompanied by a covered cart and two warriors. He met her eyes, and he didn't have to say a word for her to know of her mother's fate. A wail came from somewhere far away, and Brighid realized that it came from her.

Later, as darkness claimed the light and night fell, her mother lay in a makeshift burial mound just north of the small camp they'd made. Mael had sent word to other tribes, who'd learned of the battle and the Icenian queen's sacrifice, and they came to pay tribute as she was sent to join the gods.

Brighid stood next to Kensa and Nolwenn, tears streaking down her face. All around them, tribesmen lit their torches one by one, until torchlight illuminated the field around her mother's burial mound.

Some day I will continue your fight, Mama, Brighid silently promised her mother. *You and your sacrifice will never be forgotten.*

EPILOGUE

Lands of the Caledonian tribe
Northern Britannia
89 CE

"There lived a beast called Rome."

Nolwenn's voice was dramatic as she spoke to the children and adults who'd gathered around her. They'd heard this tale many times before, but still listened with rapt attention.

"A savage and ravenous beast, Rome had conquered most of the known world. It then turned hungry eyes across the great waters, to the wild lands of the north . . . to the lands they called Britannia. Native tribes of the land tried to fight back, to fell the beast, but they were all defeated. And like many others before them, they were forced to make an alliance. But Rome would create a beast of its own making, one that would cripple the knees of the mighty empire. Her name was Boudica . . . and she was my mother."

Brighid smiled as she watched Nolwenn from the doorway of her home. Brighid was dressed for today's battle, her face and body covered with the tribal tattoos of her adopted tribe, the Caledonians, along with the tattoos from her former tribe, the Iceni. Her gaze strayed to her two children, Mari and Peran, both adults now in their nineteenth and twentieth years. Both her children looked more like their father than her, with hair the color of wheat and clear blue eyes. They were fighting in today's battle as well, their first, but wanted to hear Nolwenn's tale of their grandmother's rebellion once more.

Nolwenn's gaze landed on Mari and Peran as she spoke, her love for them shining in her eyes. Nolwenn had chosen not to marry and joined the bard class instead, spending her days learning the tribe's history, sharing the history of the Iceni, and traveling throughout the tribal lands to tell the tale of their mother's rebellion. Her tale ensured that their mother's story would never be forgotten and inspired the Caledonians in their continual fight against the Romans.

Kensa stood on the edge of the crowd, Elouan's arm around her shoulders. She was now in her in late fifties, her golden hair shot through with gray, and Brighid's heart filled with warmth at the sight of her. She and Elouan had raised her and Nolwenn with love after Boudica's death, and even after Kensa had a brood of children of her own, she'd never felt less loved.

Brighid's thoughts turned to the upcoming battle. Her husband, Jowan, and the other warriors of the tribe already stood on the outskirts of their village, ready to meet the Roman army who marched north. Her chest tightened as she thought of the Romans. Not satisfied with southern Britannia, they now attempted to move north, to conquer the whole of the island. But her adopted tribe would never allow that. Nor would her mother, whose voice she sometimes heard in her dreams, urging her to be strong, to keep fighting.

Brighid had become a tribal warrior, one of the few women in the tribe to do so, but no one would dare protest given that she was the daughter of Boudica, the woman who'd led the most successful uprising against the Romans. She'd fought in small skirmishes against the Romans, but today's battle was against the largest Roman army she'd ever faced.

"The blood of the great warrior queen, the iron queen, Boudica, runs through my veins . . . and the veins of some of you," Nolwenn was saying, her gaze lingering on Brighid's children. "Today . . . you continue her fight."

Her audience let out raucous cheers. Mari and Peran stood to embrace Nolwenn before approaching Brighid.

"Are you certain you're ready to fight?" she asked,

the mother in her wanting them to say no, the warrior in her wanting them to say yes.

"Yes," they said in unison, and a wave of pride swept over her. They were her children—Boudica's grandchildren—indeed.

Kensa came over to embrace Brighid before they left to join the army, murmuring to her to fight well, but to be careful. Brighid gave Kensa a rueful smile.

"That's what you always say. I have grown children of my own, you know."

"Doesn't stop me from worrying," Kensa said, though she returned her smile.

After Mari and Peran said their goodbyes to Kensa, they joined the massive Caledonian army standing on the outskirts of the village. Brighid joined her husband Jowan, meeting his blue eyes with a smile.

Brighid had never intended to marry, only wanting to dedicate her life to becoming as fierce a warrior as her mother, but she'd fallen in love with Jowan in spite of herself. Jowan was a ruthless warrior, the finest of the tribe, but he was also the most compassionate man she'd ever known. Jowan gave her a wide smile and nod as their children took their places next to them.

Brighid turned to face the horizon.

At the moment, she was unaware that the day's battle would give them victory. It would stop the Romans' northward push and they would never try to conquer the north of Britannia again, and the northern tribes would live in peace. That night, her tribe would feast and celebrate, she would embrace her children and her sister, kiss her husband, and as the celebrations wound down, she would go to a stream that meandered throughout the village. She would leave a votive offering to her mother there, and tell Boudica that her fight had not been in vain. Her daughters had gone on to live full and happy lives, and they helped stop the Romans from conquering the whole of Britannia.

But Brighid didn't yet know this as the chieftain signaled for the army to charge; her focus only on the determination that coursed through her.

She raced toward the approaching Roman army, bellowing out a battle cry, the promise of victory in her heart.

THE END
of
THE IRON QUEEN

HISTORICAL NOTE

Several years ago, I heard a passing mention of a tribal queen who rebelled against the Roman Empire in the year 60 CE. Fascinated, I tucked this factoid away to the back of my mind. As I learned more about Boudica over the years, I became even more fascinated with her story. It was dramatic, vivid, emotional, and epic . . . a story I knew I had to write about.

When I began to research her story in earnest, I realized that there was not much known about the historical figure of Boudica. Much of what we do know comes to us from the Romans—her enemies—and therefore has to be taken with a grain of salt.

There are many blanks in her biography, ones which I had to fill with educated guesses—or creative license—as I worked to bring her story to life.

HISTORICAL NOTE

Antedios may or may not have been her father, there is no evidence either way, but he was chieftain of the Iceni before Prasutagus.

According to Tacitus, Boudica's rebellion happened after the death of Prasutagus. There is no evidence of what exactly killed Prasutagus. His poisoning by the Romans was my invention, though it's not too far-fetched. According to Tacitus, Catus Decianus, the procurator of Roman Britain at the time, was a greedy and unscrupulous man.

The revenge Boudica enacts against Catus and the soldiers in the novel is also creative license. Catus fled Britannia during the rebellion to relative safety in Gaul.

As for Boudica herself, Tacitus writes that Boudica poisoned herself after her army's defeat by the Romans. But after I researched the Celts, a decidedly warrior culture, that seemed unlikely to me. It seemed far more likely that she would have proudly died in battle, sacrificing herself for her cause rather than taking her own life.

The fate of Boudica's daughters after her defeat is unknown, as they disappear from the historical record. The events in the final chapter and epilogue, in which her daughters join the northern Caledonian tribes, is my invention. There were indeed battles between the Caledonians and the Romans as they pushed north, and the Romans did stop their expansion northward—most likely because it wasn't worth

HISTORICAL NOTE

the effort of fighting against the rebellious northern tribes to do so.

My portrayal of Suetonius Paulinus is much more sympathetic than the actual historical person. Suetonius was quite brutal in his attacks against the natives, so brutal that Nero had him removed as governor from Britannia after the rebellion, as he was still punishing the natives and Nero had no desire for yet another rebellion.

There is no record of Boudica and the Brigantes queen, Cartimandua, ever meeting. But she was a contemporary of Boudica's, and I couldn't resist imagining what a meeting between these two queens would have been like; one a supporter and ally of Rome, the other an ardent foe. The historical Cartimandua did outlive Boudica, though she had to flee from her lands when her people revolted against Rome in the year 69 CE, and she then disappears from the historical record.

A note about the druids. The druids were an integral part of Celtic society, much like priests and religious officials are important to many cultures today. But not much is known about them, so I had to use the few facts that do survive, such as them holding rituals in sacred groves and wearing white robes for these rituals. Someone like Mael, who is fictional in the context of this novel, would have certainly served as an advisor to a tribal chief.

The Menai massacre, the massacre the Romans

HISTORICAL NOTE

carried out against the druids on the island of Mona as punishment for inciting rebellion, actually occurred in the year 60 or 61 CE, led by Suetonius, who did have to return to the mainland when he received word of the rebellion.

A brief note about names. Brittonic, the language that Boudica and her tribe would have spoken, is a long dead language, so most of its words—and names—no longer survive. Boudica and Prasutagus's names, for example, are Latinized versions of whatever their actual Brittonic names were. This made coming up with Brittonic names for the natives tricky. I chose to use names from Celtic languages that do survive—Irish, Breton, Welsh.

I read many books and articles to immerse myself in the life of Boudica and her world. Some helpful sources include Tacitus's *The Annals* and *Boudica: Iron Age Warrior Queen* by Richard Hingley and Christina Unwin.

Bringing Boudica's powerful, tragic, yet enduring story to life was a labor of love, and I hope you enjoyed reading it as much as I enjoyed writing it.

I'd like to take a moment to thank my amazing editor Paula and my husband for always being my cheerleader and loving this story as much as I do. I'd also like to thank you, dear reader, for stepping back in time to the age of the Celts and a powerful queen who dared to defy against all odds. I hope her story inspires you in some way, as it has inspired me.

HISTORICAL NOTE

- L.G.
Los Angeles, California
2018

ALSO BY L.D. GOFFIGAN

THE MINA MURRAY SERIES

The Beast of London

Fortress of Blood

Realm of Night

Mina Murray Series Bundle: Books 1-3

ABOUT THE AUTHOR

L.D. Goffigan writes historical fiction and historical fantasy novels. She studied film and dramatic writing at New York University. Though she grew up on the East Coast, she now resides in a large glittering city by the sea on the West Coast.

She enjoys exploring fierce and complex heroes and heroines of the past and bringing them to life in the present. Her interests range from history to adventure, mysteries to thrillers–all aspects of which you'll find in her books.

When not writing, you can find her traveling to places she's never been, reading the latest book which strikes her fancy, or watching an obscure documentary about ancient past times (such documentaries do exist). And, of course, daydreaming about the next story she'll tell...

To be notified about new releases, visit L.D. Goffigan's website to sign up for her newsletter. Subscribers are also alerted to giveaways and exclusive bonus content.

Stay in touch!

www.ldgoffiganbooks.com
ld@ldgoffiganbooks.com

www.ingramcontent.com/pod-product-compliance
Lightning Source LLC
Chambersburg PA
CBHW020357080526
44584CB00014B/1054